STRUCTURE AND ORGANISATION
OF MULTINATIONAL ENTERPRISES

ORGANISATION FOR ECONOMIC CO-OPERATION AND DEVELOPMENT

Pursuant to article 1 of the Convention signed in Paris on 14th December, 1960, and which came into force on 30th September, 1961, the Organisation for Economic Co-operation and Development (OECD) shall promote policies designed:

- to achieve the highest sustainable economic growth and employment and a rising standard of living in Member countries, while maintaining financial stability, and thus to contribute to the development of the world economy;
- to contribute to sound economic expansion in Member as well as non-member countries in the process of economic development; and
- to contribute to the expansion of world trade on a multilateral, non-discriminatory basis in accordance with international obligations.

The original Member countries of the OECD are Austria, Belgium, Canada, Denmark, France, the Federal Republic of Germany, Greece, Iceland, Ireland, Italy, Luxembourg, the Netherlands, Norway, Portugal, Spain, Sweden, Switzerland, Turkey, the United Kingdom and the United States. The following countries acceded subsequently through accession at the dates hereafter: Japan (28th April, 1964), Finland (28th January, 1969), Australia (7th June, 1971) and New Zealand (29th May, 1973).

The Socialist Federal Republic of Yugoslavia takes part in some of the work of the OECD (agreement of 28th October, 1961).

Publié en français sous le titre:

STRUCTURE ET ORGANISATION
DES ENTREPRISES MULTINATIONALES

The way in which multinational enterprises organise their activities across national frontiers and the relationships between parent and subsidiary enterprises raise important issues for those involved or associated with such decisions. To what extent or in what areas are decision making structures becoming more centralised or decentralised? More generally, to what extent can the component entities of multinational enterprises have sufficient autonomy and responsibility to permit their integration into the economic context of the countries in which they operate and develop their competitive potential without impinging on the ability of the enterprise to take a global view of the company as a whole with respect to efficiency, competitiveness and profitability?

The OECD Guidelines for Multinational Enterprises address a number of recommendations to enterprises which are pertinent to these issues, and the way enterprises are structured may be relevant to the manner in which they can follow these recommendations. While the Guidelines do not call for the freezing of the structures of multinational enterprises nor infringe on the freedom of enterprises to take particular decisions in the furtherance of global strategies judged to be in the best interests of the firm as a whole, the Guidelines do contain a number of provisions relevant to the topic of this report. These are discussed in the introductory chapter.

The report analyses organisational structures and decision making patterns in multinational enterprises, as revealed by a survey of empirical research into these questions (chapter II), examines (in chapter III) the principal forces, both internal as well as external to the enterprise, determining or influencing such patterns and discusses (in chapter IV) how these patterns have been developing over time and their implications for the decision making authority in subsidiaries.

This report was approved by the Committee on International Investment and Multinational Enterprises at its June 1987 session, and was made available to the public by decision of the OECD Council on 29th September 1987.

Also available

TABLE OF CONTENTS

Chapter I

INTRODUCTION

The way in which multinational enterprises structure and organise their activities and the implications of organisational structure for the relationships between the various component entities that make up a multinational enterprise is a subject of interest for each of the main parties associated or involved with such decisions.

For the multinational enterprise, the strategic choice of a particular organisational structure and how this should develop over time is obviously a key element in the overall ability of the enterprise to maintain profitability and viability, adapt to changing circumstances and meet the needs of those who have a direct interest in the enterprise. Particularly for large multinational enterprises, operating in global markets and with many subsidiaries in a large number of countries, the organisational structure chosen is often seen as resulting from how the enterprise manages the trade-off between the need for flexibility (which is often associated with an important degree of autonomy for local units) and the need for oversight and coordination (which is often associated with the need for a certain degree of central control).

Equally, governments and labour are interested in the organisational structures of multinational enterprises, notably with respect to the position of local subsidiaries in the overall scheme of a multinational enterprise's operations. Governments and labour are obviously interested in the structure and organisation of multinational enterprises to the extent that these will influence the well-being of the local subsidiary although, in some cases the approach adopted by the enterprise might not fully reflect the desires of host governments concerning host country benefits from inward direct investment, such as the level and type of investment, employment or R&D. Equally, employee representatives have an interest in the position of the local subsidiary within the enterprise as a whole, as reflected, for example, in concerns with longer term employment stability or with access to decision makers in collective bargaining.

The topic of organisational structures in multinational enterprises and, more particularly, the situation of local subsidiaries raises a general and well-known issue – to what extent can the component entities of a multinational enterprise have sufficient responsibility to permit their integration into the economic context of the countries in which they operate, have sufficient resources to maintain and develop their competitive potential and contribute to the policy objectives of the host country without impinging on the ability of a multinational enterprise to take an overall view of the enterprise with respect to efficiency, competitiveness and profitability. In the OECD Guidelines for Multinational Enterprises, which form part of the OECD 1976 Declaration and Decisions on International Investment and Multinational Enterprises, there are a number of references which are relevant to this question.

1. Relevance of the OECD Guidelines for multinational enterprises

Initially, it is worthwhile recalling the notion of multinational enterprises on which the Guidelines are based. Paragraph 8 of the Introduction to the Guidelines states that a precise legal definition of multinational enterprises is not required for the purposes of the Guidelines. These usually comprise companies or other entities whose ownership is private, state or mixed, established in different countries and so linked that one or more of them may be able to exercise a significant influence over the activities of others and, in particular, to share knowledge and resources with the others. The degree of autonomy of each entity in relation to the others varies widely from one multinational enterprise to another, depending on the nature of the links between such entities and the fields of activity concerned. For these reasons, the Guidelines are addressed to the various entities within the multinational enterprise (parent companies and/or local entities) according to the actual distribution of responsibilities among them on the understanding that they will co-operate and provide assistance to one another as necessary to facilitate observance of the Guidelines. It may also be worth noting that the Committee on International Investment and Multinational Enterprises (the OECD Committee responsible for carrying out, inter alia, the tasks assigned to it in the OECD 1976 Declaration and Decisions on International Investment and Multinational Enterprises), has stated that, "these criteria cover a broad range of multinational activities and arrangements, which can be based on equity participation according to the traditional approach to international direct investment, but the same result could be achieved by other means not necessarily including an equity capital element. The various entities, which include parent companies, local subsidiaries, as well as intermediary levels of the organisations, are expected to co-operate and to provide assistance to one another as necessary to facilitate the observance of the Guidelines, taking into account the degree of autonomy or of dependence of each entity in practice. To the extent that parent companies actually exercise control over the activities of their subsidiaries they have a responsibility for the observance of the Guidelines by those subsidiaries"[1].

As indicated above, a number of the provisions of the General Policies chapter of the Guidelines are relevant to the topic of this report. Paragraphs 1 and 2 of the General Policies chapter recommend multinational enterprises, "to take fully into account the established general policy objectives of the Member countries in which they operate" and, in particular, "to give due consideration to those countries' aims and priorities". Paragraph 2 identifies a number of areas of aims and priorities. Paragraph 5 of the General Policies chapter of the Guidelines recommends enterprises to, "allow their component entities freedom to develop their activities and to exploit their competitive advantage in domestic and foreign markets, consistent with the need for specialisation and sound commercial practice".

In the 1979 Review Report on the 1976 Declaration and Decisions on International Investment and Multinational Enterprises[2], the Committee stated that paragraph 5 of the General Policies (read together with paragraph 4 of the same chapter which recommends favouring close cooperation with the local community and business interests) can be understood to be in favour of a certain degree of integration of the component entities of a multinational enterprise into the economic context of the countries in which they operate. On the other hand, the insertion of the words "consistent with the need for specialisation and sound commercial practices" in paragraph 5 was intended to provide for giving due consideration to the interests of a multinational enterprise as a whole, as well as the situation of any of its entities. The Guidelines do not call for the freezing of the existing structures of multinational enterprises nor do they infringe the freedom of multinational enterprises to take decisions to divest in the furtherance of global strategies judged to be in the best interests of the firm as a whole. But this freedom is circumscribed according to national law and contractual obligations entered into by firms and affected by paragraphs 1 and 2 of the chapter on General Policies (which recommend enterprises to take fully into account established general policies of the Member countries in which they operate and to give due consideration to particular aims and priorities).

As recalled in the 1984 Review Report on the Declaration and Decisions[3], the Guidelines may be understood as recommending that enterprises should favour, to the extent possible, integration of the component entities of a multinational enterprise into the economic context of countries in which they operate, and that they should provide these entities will sufficient responsibilities and resources to enable them to maintain and develop their competitive potential, giving due concern to the interests of the enterprise as a whole as well as the situation of any of its entities. These considerations may allow entities greater opportunities for competitive structural adjustment, as opposed to contraction, when realistic choices exist, and to engage in adjustments that may be important for some governments such as developing and utilising economic local sources of supply, upgrading natural resources before export and allowing local equity participation.

A number of the recommendations of the chapter of the Guidelines on Employment and Industrial Relations also have a bearing on the subject of this report. For example, in the context of negotiations between management and labour on collective bargaining or labour-management relations issues, which is addressed in paragraph 9 of the Employment and Industrial Relations chapter of the Guidelines, the Committee has noted that when negotiations or collective bargaining are proceeding in the context of any parent-subsidiary relationship, there is clearly a possibility that the subsidiary may not be fully empowered to negotiate and to conclude an agreement. There may be special problems in the case of a subsidiary which is situated in one country whilst the parent company is situated in another. The purpose of the text of the Guidelines is to lay stress on the access of employee representatives to management representataives "who are authorised to take decisions on the matters under negotiation". This is the key consideration and the management of a multinational enterprise should see that it is observed in the circumstances of each case. The Committee has also stated that parent companies are expected to take the necessary organisational steps to enable their subsidiaries to observe the Guidelines, inter alia, by providing them with adequate and timely information and ensuring that their representatives who carry out negotiations at the national or local level have sufficient authority to take decisions on the matters under negotiation[4].

Also, it is the view of the Committee that general provisions of the Guidelines, such as paragraphs 1 and 8 of the Introduction together with item i) of the chapter on Disclosure of Information (which concerns the structure of the enterprise), could not be seen to imply a general right of employees to be informed on the decision-making structure within the enterprise. It is agreed, however, that it is the basic purpose of paragraph 9 of the Employment and Industrial Relations chapter of the Guidelines to ensure that negotiations take place in a meaningful manner with the relevant representataives of management. For this purpose employee representataives, under the Guidelines, have a legitimate interest to be informed about the decision-making structure within the enterprise but such a right of information is confined to negotiating situations referred to in the Guidelines, and in particular in paragraph 9 of the Chapter on Employment and Industrial Relations of the Guidelines[5].

2. General considerations

Before examining the patterns of multinational enterprises behaviour as revealed by the literature on the subject (discussed in Chapter II) and their development over time (Chapter IV) and the forces determining or influencing such patterns (discussed in Chapter III), it is appropriate to set the discussion in perspective by first considering a number of more general points, related to the basic position that organisational structures and parent-subsidiary relationships in multinational enterprises, influenced as they are by a very large variety of forces, are often complex and fluid and that each enterprise selects its particular approach on the basis of its own situation and, as the latter changes, so too can changes be expected in how it organises its activities.

First of all, there are many different types of multinational enterprises, different means of establishing foreign operations, different approaches to international involvement and different broad approaches to organisational structure. For example, multinational enterprises can vary from those of a very limited nature, such as having only one or two foreign subsidiaries producing similar goods to those of global proportions with numerous subsidiaries in many countries producing goods or services for very different markets. Similarly, in establishing foreign operations, this may be done by new greenfield investments or by the acquisition of existing domestic firms while the nature of involvement may range from full or majority equity positions to what is often called "new forms of international involvement, these being characterised by minority or even no equity involvement.[6] As to the main forms of organisational structures adopted, particularly by larger multinational enterprises, these are generally of two broad types, functional and multidivisional. Functional structures divide the organisation globally along functional lines such as purchasing, marketing and finance, which are separated and coordinated for the enterprise's global operations. The multidivisional structure involves the organisation of all corporate functions along product and/or geographic lines where, for example, a regional headquarters might coordinate all of the functional areas for its region and report to the parent enterprise. Within these two broad approaches there are obviously many variations as to intensity and mix, reflecting the particular needs of the enterprise for coordinating and controlling its various activities in the markets in which it operates.

The position of the foreign located subsidiary in the enterprise as a whole, particularly with respect to its voice in various decisions, is a complex and often ambiguous area. Although this topic is frequently discussed in terms of centralised/decentralised decision making, it is clear that the polar situations of total centralisation or full autonomy do not exist. In any multinational enterprise, indeed in any multiplant enterprise, it can be expected that the environment in which it operates generates forces, some of which go in the direction of more centralised coordination and control while others, particularly when related to the need for local knowledge, experience and flexibility go in the direction of greater local autonomy. The task of the enterprise is then to develop a means or structure to manage and resolve these often competing forces.

The actual choice of organisational structure adopted by the enterprise can be difficult to discern or interpretate. For example, more complex organisations function along multiple dimensions and what may appear to be a highly centralised structure, as seen from an organigram, may turn out to be quite uncoordinated in its actual functions, or highly centralised procedures for coordinating long term strategic decisions may be accompanied by loosely coordinated implementation. Also, coordination of one function within a company does not imply coordination of another. On the other hand, of course, authors such as Brooke and Black[7] have concluded that an ideology of decentralisation was sometimes masking a reality of centralisation. These authors interviewed managers of the head office of international companies who all said that the policy was to decentralise. During the same period, however, a majority of subsidiary executives affirmed that the opposite was taking place. Further investigations by these authors usually confirmed the latter view rather than the former. Obviously, the terms decentralisation or autonomy, as well as a number of other terms used in the present report, can be used in a number of different senses, as witnessed in the variety of empirical studies referred to in chapters II to IV below, which have been conducted by authors of many different nationalities and which cover different samples of multinational enterprises (in terms of, for example, nationality of the parent company, location of subsidiaries, sample size and constitution, etc.).

In discussing the significance of the locus of decision making authority, a Conference Board study[8], which is based on the responses by 109 companies to a survey, points to a number of caveats to be borne in mind. For example, it is stated that the exercise of authority is highly personal and situational with companies dealing with component units on a case by case basis, and the need for parental approval can mean anything from direct instructions to passive ratification. Even in cases of significant local autonomy, the manager may not choose to use his full decision making authority, for example due to lack of knowledge at the local level or because it is politically prudent to involve headquarters. In any event, an important role is played in the distribution of decision making power by the personality of the local manager and his successfulness.

Not only should the degree of parent control or influence be seen as a spectrum, but also it has to be borne in mind that corporate management has at its disposal a range of means for implementing the level of influence it wishes to have over subsidiaries' activities. One group of such mechanisms includes direct instructions to the subsidiary, the definition of limitations on its zone of autonomy, such as thresholds for financial expenditure below which the subsidiary has full authority, and the use of specifications, standardised procedures and management methods to be used enterprise-wide. Also falling into this group are practices such as product mandating, whereby the parent company may place restrictions on the products to be produced in a subsidiary and the market or markets in which they can be sold. Thus, while marketing decisions, as will be seen below, are frequently the responsibility of the local subsidiary given the need for flexibility and local knowledge, the use of such practices places constraints on the zone of autonomy exercised at the subsidiary level. Apart from the above there are a number of other, more indirect means of ensuring compatibility between subsidiary activities and corporate strategies. These methods may include, for example, the use of expatriates in key positions and the use of intra-company visits, they may relate to the nature and frequency of reporting obligations or, more generally, the development of an enterprise wide culture, defined as an internal value system and identity with the company achieved by a series of general principles and norms shared throughout the company. The general objective behind such mechanisms is to ensure that decisions taken at the local level take account of company-wide objectives. An important implication of the means used to ensure this compatibility is that, depending on the nature or mix of methods used, they can act in certain situations to blur the distinction between central and local decision making.

A further important point to note is that there are both different types or levels of decisions as well as links between different decisions. Studies investigating the decision making process in complex organisations generally divide decisions into two broad groups – strategic and operational. Strategic decisions determine the general orientation of the activity of the enterprise or, more generally of the organisation and include decisions such as the addition of a new product line, diversification, upstream or downstream integration, internationalisation, restructuing, acquisition, disinvestment and the adoption of new technologies. Operational decisions generally relate to the day to day management of activity and generally involve a degree of freedom and margin for initiative at the level of the local subsidiary. Such decisions can include decisions relating to, for example, production levels, marketing and advertising and employment and personnel policy. Obviously decisions in all of these areas are linked in the sense that they reflect overall strategy and how this is implemented. Aside from this, decisions may be linked in the sense that decisions on, for example, investment, production and technology will influence decisions on employment. If, as is sometimes the case, decisions of the former type are taken centrally while the latter are taken by the local subsidiary, strategic decisions can define the limits or parameters within which operational decisions are taken. As noted above, central control in one decision area does not imply similar control in a different area, yet this must be seen in the perspective of the links that may exist between different decision areas.

Also, the literature on this subject often gives a rather static picture of organisational patterns in multinational enterprises by taking snapshots of certain relationships between the parent and its subsidiaries and then suggesting general conclusions about the overall behaviour of the multinational enterprise. Although researchers draw attention to the fact that different types of relationships exist, often little or no account is taken of the possible short term and sometimes temporary changes in specific areas, as opposed to more major and longer term orientations. For example, temporary scarcity or shifts in prices of raw materials can bring about temporary changes in the central/local purchasing relationship, or large exchange rate fluctuations may bring about temporary changes in attitude by the parent company in financial matters which otherwise are left to the subsidiary. Also, the perceived financial position or short term outlook for a multinational enterprise as a whole can bring about temporary changes in the delegation of responsibility for capital expenditure from the parent company to the subsidiary.

Finally, it can be noted that many of these analyses take what Ghertman[9] calls the "centralisation-decentralisation" approach – namely asking executives which decisions are made by the parent, made by the subsidiary or shared. In many cases, such studies concentrate on factors internal to the organisation in explaining observed patterns (see chapter III, 1) with often less than adequate treatment given to particular internal aspects such as general strategic objectives, management philosophy and personalities. The general results of such investigations often reveal particular characteristics associated with the division of decision making authority, although many internal characteristics either seem to play a minimum role or provide results which are too variable to be convincing. A more general lacunae in such studies is that they tend to minimise factors external to the organisation, particularly the political and economic context in which they operate (see chapter III, 2).

Indeed, in Ghertman's view the question of how management at different levels of the organisational structure interact, particularly with respect to strategic decisions, may be more important than that of whether the parent or the subsidiary takes a particular decision. This view sees decision making as an iterative process which can be bottom-up or top-down, but where in any event decisions go through various phases (initiation, impetus, trial,) and iterations between management levels before the end decision is made and implemented. While it is often easy to pinpoint when a particular decision comes to an end, e.g. the closure of a plant, an advantage of seeing decision making as a process, is that it may provide insight into when the events leading to a particular decision emerge and how the decision is reached. In general, however, work on this analytical approach is still largely at the conceptual phase, with investigation being restricted to a small number of case studies.

Chapter II

MULTINATIONAL ENTERPRISE PRACTICES WITH RESPECT TO SUBSIDIARY RELATIONS

Whereas the legal relationships between parent company and subsidiary are usually clear, the problem faced by researchers investigating decision making structures in large and complex enterprises is to penetrate the complicated network of coalitions and subcoalitions which make up the organisation and whose inter-relationships determine how it actually works. In the empirical literature two basic approaches have been used. One is to identify the locus of decision making, an approach which tries to find techniques for allocating decision making within a company and thus determine in some way an index of centralisation. Another approach is through the power structure – an attempt to determine where power lies, how much power is shared, and how real this power sharing is. Both types of approaches normally use perceptual measures. Although this might seem to be a drawback, a number of studies have indicated, however, that in terms of behaviour, perception is reality.

While a brief reference will be made to functional areas studies, most of the studies surveyed and referred to in this section use the locus of decision-making approach. In these studies decentralisation means autonomy with respect to various decisions. For example, autonomy can be related to the hiring and firing of personnel, finance decisions, marketing strategies and production decisions. More recent studies, such as those of Welge and Negandhi[10] and Welge[11], assess subsidiary autonomy in such a way that a catalogue of different decisions is developed, covering the most important corporate functions. For each item, the chief executive officer of the subsidiary evaluates the influence of the subsidiary on the particular decision, and also the influence of corporate headquarters on that decision. The decisions selected are both operational as well as strategic in nature.

Table 1.   CORRELATION COEFFICIENTS BY DECISION-MAKING AREAS

	1	2	3	4
1. Expenditure control (financial decisions)	—	0.46	0.14	0.10
2. Exporting policy decisions.....................	—	—	0.15	0.14
3. Pricing policy decisions	—	—	—	0.15
4. Setting of targets............................	—	—	—	—

Source: Abell, 1974, p. 14.
Note: The correlation coefficient between any two decision areas (e.g., item 1, expenditure control and item 2, exporting policy decisions, 0.46) shows the level of association between these two variables. The closer is the correlation coefficient to 1.00 the closer is the association between the two variables.

The findings of an early study by Alsegg[12] which used the functional area approach, suggest that the degree of autonomy granted to foreign subsidiaries of United States companies differs between functional areas such as marketing, production and finance. While this study is more qualitative in nature, Abell's[13] findings indicate that control in one area of decision making by no means guarantees control in another area. The correlation coefficients between different decision-making areas are very low, as seen from Table 1.

A comprehensive empirical study on the autonomy of foreign subsidiaries using the decision area approach was carried out by Hedlund[14]. In this survey, interviews in 77 subsidiaires of 39 parents in the United States, the United Kingdom, Germany, Japan and Sweden were conducted. The results are presented in Tables 2 and 3.

From Table 2 it can be inferred that the 77 foreign subsidiaries investigated enjoy a great deal of decision autonomy for many types of decision. A score between "4" and "5" indicates that a typical subsidiary may decide on the issue after consultation with the headquarters or may even decide independently. A score scarcely below "5" shows that on the average most subsidiaries have the sole say in these decisions. Typical decisions for which this holds true are the hiring and firing of workers, the responsibility for collective wage bargaining, transfer of employees between departments, taking disciplinary actions, and choice of advertising agencies. These results provide a first impression of the types of decisions or functional areas in which a high degree of autonomy can be expected, a question which is further discussed below.

The least degree of autonomy was observed for decisions concerning return-on-investment (ROI) criteria, dividend policy, royalty payments and central overhead costs, and choice of public accountants. The score for these decision areas means that on average the headquarter decides alone or after consultation with the subsidiary. Nevertheless, the average score of 3.67 on the 5-point scale indicates a considerable amount of autonomy on the side of the subsidiary. Normally, on average, the subsidiary either decides itself on the various issues but the decisions are subject to approval by the headquarters, or the subsidiary decides itself only after consultation with headquarters.

Table 3 presents a condensed and slightly different result of the Hedlund study. But here again decisions concerning e.g. choice of public accountant and financial issues, introduction of new products and increase of production capacity, which might be regarded as strategic decisions, are highly centralised at the headquarter level, while subsidiaries enjoy the highest degree of autonomy with decisions on personnel.

Driving the process of condensing of the data another step further permits a differentiation of subsidiary autonomy for various management functions (see Table 4). These results confirm the impressions resulting from the information provided above; for personnel decisions, subsidiary autonomy is the highest, whereas for finance decisions, it is lowest. An intermediate position is held by production and marketing decisions. The distinction between decisions of strategic and global overall importance and relevance on the one hand and operational decisions on the other may explain these results to some extent.

Summarising the results reported, the Hedlund study found that for most decisions the influence of the subsidiary is greater than that of the headquarters. Despite that, the results seem to point to the conclusion that headquarters have a considerable say on specific kinds of decisions which may be classified as follows:

a) Decisions that draw on or directly affect central resources,

e.g. – use of expatriate personnel;
– expansion of production capacity;
– raising equity capital;

Table 2. SUBSIDIARY AUTONOMY FOR DIFFERENT TYPES OF DECISIONS

	Decision area	Score
1.	Change of subsidiary organisation	3.47
2.	Hiring top management in subsidiary	3.32
3.	Salary level for top management in subsidiary	3.18
4.	Hiring and firing of workers	4.97
5.	Payment routines for employee wages	4.78
6.	Responsibility for collective wage bargaining	4.97
7.	Training programme in subsidiary	4.60
8.	Transfer of employees between departments	4.88
9.	Restructuring of work tasks	4.86
10.	Taking disciplinary action (warnings, fines, etc.)	4.97
11.	Security against industrial espionage	4.60
12.	Extent of over-time work	5.00
13.	Vacations for employees not legally fixed	4.40
14.	Choice of suppliers	4.18
15.	Purchasing methods	4.54
16.	Yearly production volume	3.40
17.	Increase in production capacity	2.62
18.	Quality control norms	3.36
19.	Changes in manufacturing process	3.65
20.	Maintenance of production facilities	4.66
21.	Choice of costing system	2.85
22.	Decision on work efficiency studies	4.84
23.	Choice of work methods	4.68
24.	Entering new markets within country	3.75
25.	Entering new markets outside country	2.24
26.	Introduction of new products	2.79
27.	Choice of distribution channels	3.79
28.	Adaptation of standard products	4.05
29.	Setting sales targets	3.17
30.	Preparing market plans	3.84
31.	Level of advertising budget	4.16
32.	Choice of advertising agency	4.88
33.	Pricing of products sold locally	4.19
34.	Delivery times or order priorities	4.84
35.	Customer credit	4.25
36.	Product design	3.49
37.	Advertising approach	4.35
38.	Preparing financial plans	3.03
39.	Return on investment criteria	1.85
40.	Loans from local banks	3.08
41.	Raising equity capital	1.48
42.	Dividend policy	1.54
43.	Royalty payments and central overhead costs	1.77
44.	Use of cash-flow in subsidiary	2.49
45.	Choice of public accountant	1.91
46.	Spending unbudgeted capital on investments	2.31
47.	Organisation of budget work	3.07
48.	International transfer prices	3.24
	Average	3.67

Source: Hedlund, 1981, p. 29.
Sample of 77 subsidiaries of 39 multinational enterprises.
Note: Using a scale of 1 (low autonomy) to 5 (high autonomy) the following "scores" can be interpreted as follows:
1 = Decided by HQ alone
2 = Decided by HQ after consultation with subsidiary
3 = Decided by subsidiary but subject to approval by HQ
4 = Decided by subsidiary after consultation with HQ
5 = Decided independently by subsidiary.

Table 3. DEGREE OF AUTONOMY BY TYPE OF DECISION IN THE INTERVIEW

	Rank	Score
Choice of public accountant	1	1.91
Use of cash flow in subsidiary	2	2.49
Increase of production capacity	3	2.62
Introduction of new product	4	2.79
Loans from local banks	5	3.08
Appointing CEO, Top management personnel	6	3.32
Determining product volume for the year	7	3.40
Pricing of products sold in local market	8	4.19
Customer credit	9	4.25
Personnel training programme for subsidiary	10	4.60
Maintenance of facilities	11	4.66
Choice of advertising agency	12	4.88
Hiring and firing of workers	13	4.97
Average score		3.62

Source: Hedlund, 1981, p. 38
Note: See the note to Table 2.
Decision areas ranked in descending order of centralisation.
Sample of 66 multinational enterprises.

Table 4. SUBSIDIARY AUTONOMY FOR VARIOUS MANAGEMENT FUNCTIONS

	Average	Range
Personnel decisions (1-13 in Table 2)	4.45	3.18-5.00
Production decisions (14-23 in Table 2)	3.96	2.62-4.84
Marketing decisions (24-37 in Table 2)	3.82	2.24-4.88
Finance decisions (38-48 in Table 2)	2.38	1.48-3.25

Source: Hedlund, 1981.
Note: Using a scale of 1 (low autonomy) to 5 (high autonomy) the following "scores" can be interpreted as follows:
1 = Decided by HQ alone
2 = Decided by HQ after consultation with subsidiary
3 = Decided by subsidiary but subject to approval by HQ
4 = Decided by subsidiary after consultation with HQ
5 = Decided independently by subsidiary.

       – dividend policy;
       – determination of royalties and administration fees.

b) Decisions which constitute long-term obligations.

c) Decisions to ensure standardisation and a common framework of organisational routines and practices throughout the company,

    e.g.   – choice of public accountant;
          – transfer pricing policies;
          – quality control norms;
          – choice of cost systems;
          – product designs.

Table 5. AUTONOMY OF SUBSIDIARY MANAGERS
WITH RESPECT TO VARIOUS BUSINESS INSTRUMENTS

QUESTION: Instruments. From the point of view of the overall corporation, relatively how independent are the managers of foreign and domestic subsidiaries engaged in international transfers with respect to each of the following business policy instruments?

Decision area	Percent of sample				Mean	Std. Dev.
	Subsidiary determines		Parent determines			
	Entirely	Mostly	Mostly	Entirely		
1. Physical quantities produced ..	40	31	23	6	3.058	0.938
2. Price on sales to subsidiaries in same country	29	42	15	13	2.865	0.991
3. Price on sales to subsidiaries in other countries..........	19	29	37	15	2.519	0.980
4. Price on sales outside company	38	50	8	4	3.231	0.757
5. Quantity of items sold to other subsidiaries	27	40	23	10	2.846	0.937
6. Quantity of items purchased from other subsidiaries	27	42	27	4	2.923	0.837
7. Materials and labour purchased in the open market	35	60	4	2	3.269	0.630
8. Major capital investments	0	10	56	35	1.750	0.622
9. Dividends remitted to parent company	0	12	37	52	1.596	0.693
10. Major borrowings	0	10	42	48	1.615	0.661
11. Marketing expenditures	13	60	17	10	2.769	0.807
12. Research and development expenditures	4	31	35	29	2.098	0.878

Source: Yunker, 1983.
The percentage response indicates the division of decision making responsibility by each of the 12 decision areas listed.
Note: Percent is adjusted to nearest whole number.
Sample size is 52 corporations.

The results of the study by Yunker[15] point in the same direction. In 52 corporations she investigated, among other things, the autonomy of subsidiary managers with respect to various business instruments. In this study, the findings of which are presented in Table 5, managers of subsidiaries engaged in international transfer had least independence with respect to major capital investments, dividends remitted to the parent company, major borrowing, and research and development expenditures, decision areas which Yunker calls long-run instruments. The highest independence of subsidiary management was found in the category of short-run instruments such as decisions with respect to materials and labour purchased in the open market, price on sales outside the company and physical quantities produced.

The findings and conclusions of the two forementioned studies are supported by those of studies by Brandt and Hulbert[16] and Alpander[17]. The former examined "headquarters guidance" in the marketing function, a theoretical construction which is not absolutely identical with the concept of autonomy but which characterises parent involvement in subsidiary decision making and which is therefore closely related to the concept of autonomy.

17

The authors were able to show that headquarters guidance was particularly high in product-related areas such as product-design specifications, brand name and package design. Taking into account that this study focuses only on the marketing function, parent involvement is high in areas which are of greatest importance for the multinational enterprise as a whole, e.g. for presenting a consistent image in all markets and regions in which the company is operating.

Alpander's study which investigated home-base-affiliate relations in 64 multinational enterprises, points in the same direction. According to this study, labour negotiations turned out to be the least centralised function with employment planning, technical and supervisory training, recruitment and selection only slightly more centralised. At the other end of the spectrum, management training and salary administration seem to be more centrally controlled. Control by corporate headquarters was particularly high in the finance and accounting areas while most accounting functions and expansion planning are routinely performed centrally. However, one should also bear in mind that such results cannot be taken to mean, for example, that important decisions concerning labour negotiations are always decentralised or that all the decisions in the finance or accounting area are taken by headquarters.

The Conference Board study referred to in chapter I[18] investigated decision making patterns in 109 companies (of United States, Canadian and European origin) and their subsidiaries and compared the patterns found for particular decision areas with features of the enterprise and its activity such as whether the company was single or multiple business related, organised on geographic or product lines, capital or labour intensive or technology or consumer orientated. The broad results of this investigation, summarised in table 6, are as follows. Parent retention of authority for capital expenditure decisions is uniformly high for all types of companies, this being the area where corporations are especially zealous in guarding their prerogatives, but it was also found that local managers of single businesses are less likely to need parental approval to build a new plant. For the selection of top personnel, companies which are single product or capital intensive are more likely to insist on parental approval than in companies organised on geographic lines or which are more highly internationally orientated. Territorial or jurisdictional issues such as entry into a new country are likely to involve greater parent influence in companies evenly divided between geographic and product lines, and as the percentage of foreign to total business increases, the need for approval increases significantly. In the area of new product introduction, parental approval is more likely to be required in companies organised along both geographic and product lines and companies which are not highly labour or capital intensive, in comparison to their more homogenous counterparts. Labour relations decisions, generally quite autonomous, and establishing R&D facilities, generally quite centralised, display little variation among these different types of companies, although, with respect to R&D facilities, this is likely to be even more so the case in geographic organisations and labour intensive firms.

Young, Hood and Hamill[19] examined the divisions in decision making responsibilities in 154 foreign subsidiaries (mostly of American or European origin) located in the United Kingdom. Like other earlier studies of the situation in the United Kingdom[20] they found that financial decisions were among the most centralised, but noted important distinctions between different types of financial decisions. For example, dividend and royalty payments, financial targets and return on investment targets were found to be areas typical of central decision authority whereas the choice of capital investment projects and their financing appear to be more decentralised, with a strong, decisive parent influence only exerted in a minority of cases. In respect of the latter types of decision, the authors noted that the majority of such projects were small, falling within financial limits set by the parent. Nevertheless, it was felt that, on

Table 6. DECISION-MAKING AUTHORITY IN LOCAL UNITS

Decision area	Number of operations where local or regional unit has		
	Full authority	Authority to take action, but must consult with higher level	Authority to recommend; parent must approve any major action
Capital expenditures			
Acquire local business......................	3	19	299
(Local interests control)	5	14	59
Enter joint venture	4	30	288
(Local interests control)	5	17	56
Build new plant	8	24	285
(Local interests control)	4	21	52
Miscellaneous			
Build research facility	16	63	255
(Local interests control)	9	24	46
Top personnel issues			
Choose new director	9	74	241
(Local interests control)	6	30	40
Select new head	15	78	226
(Local interests control)	7	34	37
Territorial and jurisdictional issues			
Enter new territory	7	60	241
(Local interests control)	6	20	48
Business decisions			
Product introduction........................	62	98	150
(Local interests control)	17	25	32
Labour and external relations			
Discuss political issues	60	186	68
(Local interests control)	22	38	14
Negotiate labour contract....................	175	124	15
(Local interests control)	57	19	5

Source: Conference Board, 1983.
Note: Sample of 109 companies.
For each decision area, level of authority in local or regional unit given for two situations, where local interests (particularly 8 host governments) do not have a controlling interest and (in parenthesis) where they do exert a controlling interest.

the basis of other work by these authors[21] that there is considerable variety in project appraisal at parent company level. Overall, therefore, it was felt that, in contrast with the results relating to overseas companies in other countries (for example, that for Belgium, discussed below), the United Kingdom subsidiaries of multinational enterprises appear to be granted a substantial degree of autonomy in most financial decisions, including those concerning capital investment.

In the other decision areas investigated, the findings parallel those already reported above. For example, R&D was found to be not only centrally controlled at the corporate level, but also typically centrally located. Operational decisions in the production and marketing sphere typically displayed a high degree of autonomy, except with respect to decisions concerning the entry into non-United Kingdom markets and markets supplied by the United Kingdom subsidiary, the latter illustrating the product mandating practices as discussed in chapter I. Similarly, employment and personnel decisions were generally among the most decentralised areas. A low level of parent company involvement in areas such as union recognition and collective bargaining was found, although Hamill[22] has suggested that parent enterprises may exert a strong indirect influence through company-wide codes and guidelines.

In connection with the latter point – indirect parent influence – the study by Young, Hood and Hamill examined various means of indirect control such as the use of expatriate personnel, information flows and intra-company visits but, at least in comparison to other similar studies, their results did not suggest that such indirect mechanisms were all that substantial.

A number of the conclusions reached in a study of foreign-controlled enterprises in Belgium by Van Den Bulke and Halsberghe[23] are quite different from those reported above in the United Kingdom study. These authors felt that the subsidiaries examined were generally not able to take investment decisions independently. In addition, about one-third of the subsidiaries felt that capital expenditure ceilings implied tight control in their cases and, indeed, in 70 per cent of the cases it was found that capital ceilings had remained relatively fixed for some time, implying a real decline in these ceilings. In the area of product quality and composition, decisions were found to be totally determined by the parent in one-quarter of the cases and decisively by the parent in half of the cases. As concerns marketing, which is an interesting area in that there is a need for flexibility to adapt to local circumstances together with a need to organise operations to exploit advantages from integrated unified strategies, the study found that one-third of the subsidiaries had exclusive responsibility while a further one-third took the final decision after consultation with the parent. The authors noted that marketing authority may be limited by export restrictions where it was found that about two-thirds of United States, United Kingdom and Dutch subsidiaries and half or more of the French and German subsidiaries were not allowed to export back to the home country and also sometimes to markets close to the home country. Employment and related decisions were found to be the most decentralised, particularly because of the need to take account of the specific industrial relations system of the host country.

In looking at the role played by the degree of multinationality, Van den Bulke and Halsberghe distinguish between emerging multinationals (which are relatively small with only a few subsidiaries in two or three countries) and global multinationals (which are very large, with many subsidiaries in many countries and where a significant proportion of total production is outside the home country). Intermediate stages between these extremes are referred to as multinational orientated companies. These authors found that financial decisions are supervised most thoroughly in emerging multinationals, while this type of enterprise also has a more pronounced and stricter control pattern for employment decisions. More generally, it was found that while direct headquarter control increases as the degree of multinationality decreases, the reverse pattern is found for indirect monitoring devices such as reporting and intracompany visits.

In comparison to the United Kingdom study noted above, indirect influence was felt to be more significant. While there is a long history of host country nationals in key posts in the United Kingdom, expatriates typically held such positions in the subsidiaries in Belgium, although it was noted that this was particularly so in the case of new establishments and that this gradually decreased over time. The frequency of intra-company visits was found to parallel the importance to the company of the different decision areas. As the authors point out, the main reasons for such visits were to exchange information and evaluate subsidiary performance, but that the visits do not represent a "one-way traffic" in the sense that they also provide subsidiary personnel with the opportunity to impress headquarters.

As can be expected from the general discussion of chapter I, a conclusion emerging from the above studies is the obvious one that the parent company is likely to play a greater role in those decisions which are of importance to the overall strategy of the company. In this respect, the distinction between strategic and operational decisions and the levels at which they are taken becomes important, but as the above discussion indicates, even for strategic decisions there are often important differences with respect to the relative role played by the parent and the subsidiary or the manner in which the parent achieves the degree of influence felt required. As pointed out by Ghertman[24] therefore, the type of decision is an important factor in explaining the division of responsibility, but the diversity of practices for a given decision, as noted above, suggests that there are also other factors playing important roles, and it is to these that the discussion now turns.

Chapter III

FACTORS DETERMINING
AND INFLUENCING ORGANISATIONAL STRUCTURE

This chapter looks at the various factors which can be expected to determine or at least influence the organisational structures of multinational enterprises and the manner in which particular decisions are made. These forces are divided into two broad groups. First, the role of factors internal to the enterprise and concerning various characteristics of the parent or organisation as a whole, the subsidiary and interrelations between these are examined. Second, the external environment in which the enterprise operates is discussed, focusing on three broad sets of factors – the economic climate, technology and government policy.

1. Factors internal to the enterprise

In all business operations, risk is an important factor. In the context of multinational operations, some risk elements are of a general character and result from the situation of the parent company in having foreign operations. Other risks are specific to a given environment and therefore will differ from one foreign affiliate to another. The former risk elements are amenable to a general policy whereas the latter have to be treated specifically for each affiliate. Thus, as Garnier[25] notes, the actual degree of autonomy granted to a given affiliate will reflect both the general policies set by the parent company for all its foreign affiliates and the specific conditions that characterise this affiliate. According to this, contextual factors can be grouped in categories, which should be investigated separately, related to the characteristics of the parent company or the whole multinational enterprise-system, (such as industry, nationality, size, degree of internationalisation, and aspects of corporate strategy) and characteristics of the specific subsidiary (such as country of location, size, performance, and age). In addition, it is also useful to examine as a separate category aspects of the links between the parent and subsidiary such as the manner of subsidiary establishment or degree of ownership and the level of interdependence between the activities of the parent and other entities in the group.

a) *Characteristics of the group or parent company*

   – *Industry and related aspects*

A study by Egelhoff[26] found that the average degree of autonomy differs between industrial groups, a finding in accordance with that of other studies such as those by Alsegg[27], Garnier[28] and Brooke and Remmers[29]. From these it appears that the automobile, industrial equipment, and tyre industries tend to have relatively high levels of autonomy of output and behavioural control, while the findings of Brandt and Hulbert[30] indicate a moderate amount of headquarter guidance in the pharmaceutical and chemical, the office equipment and the textile industries. No or little relationship could be observed in consumer packaged goods, motor vehicles and major components, and electrical and telecommunications industries. Also, Kenter[31] observed for the latter a high level of planned autonomy in the personnel area. As noted earlier, it might be expected that the specific characteristics of particular industrial sectors, for example, food and related products or pharmaceuticals, would lead to relatively high levels of local autonomy in areas such as marketing. For example, important differences between countries with respect to tastes or product legislation require high levels of local knowledge and responsiveness, yet such a sector-specific relationship is not always found. This being said, therefore, it seems that industry type is not a major indicator explaining differences in autonomy levels. In fact, and , as suggested in studies by Kenter and Welge[32], Kenter[33] and Gaydoul[34] a focus on industry type clouds the main explanatory factors and intermingles their influences. As Garnier[35] suggested, it is thus necessary to go beyond these superficial elements to determine the specific causes of differences.

Other aspects related to industry characteristics, such as the competitive situation may influence relations between parent and subsidiary. For example, if there is only local competition on the local market, decentralisation may be the most likely approach, but if global competitors come in, who intend to transfer marketing results quickly from one country to another, the parent company may take a different view about the subsidiary's autonomy. What looks like a local product introduction could be the beginning of a competitor's move in the whole region. If one competitor takes this approach the market will change dramatically and the main parties will have to follow suit if they do not wish to be left behind. These factors may change the parent-subsidiary relationship temporarily or basically and not only in the marketing area.

– Company type

The study by the Conference Board[36], which examined various decision areas according to features of the company, found a number of relationships between such company characteristics and the general approach towards delegation and local control, the results of which are summarised in Table 7. For example, companies organised along product lines generally retain greater central authority over decisions on key personnel as each of the entities is in fact part of a network and it is important that subsidiaries fit well into this network. In comparison, companies organised along geographic lines may see themselves more as a federation of local companies, associated, therefore, with greater degree of local autonomy. In the area of product introduction, there may be greater central involvement in single product as opposed to multiproduct companies, as in the former, control over how the product is marketed may be of vital importance whereas the image of multiproduct companies is more diverse, depending on a variety of products.

– Nationality

A study by Hedlund[37] sheds some first light on the influence of nationality of the parent company. Table 8 shows the results of the comparison of the respective degrees of influence of subsidiaries and headquarters of Swedish, United States and Japanese multinational enterprises, averaged over 15 different decisions. It can be seen that Swedish subsidiaries are considerably more autonomous than the subsidiaries of United States multinational enterprises and slightly more autonomous than the subsidiaries of Japanese multinationals. As the

Table 7. GENERAL APPROACH TO DELEGATION OF AUTHORITY

Characteristics of companies	General approach to delegation
Geographic and product line companies	Product-line companies retain more authority for top personnel decisions.
Single and multi-product business	Single-product companies are more likely to retain authority for product introduction.
Consumer and technology producing companies	Technology-producing companies give local manager more authority for political decisions. Consumer companies more likely to require consultation before entering new territory.
Capital—and labour—intensive companies	In labour-intensive companies local manager is more likely to have greater authority to establish research or development facility.
Percentage of foreign business	Companies with more than 50 percent foreign business more likely to retain parental authority over local political issues.

Source: Conference Board, 1983.
Note: For each of the company characteristics subject to comparison (e.g., companies organised along geographic versus product lines, for single versus multiple product companies, etc.) the table describes differences in the general approach to delegation.

Table 8. INFLUENCE OF SUBSIDIARIES AND HEADQUARTERS
OF SWEDISH, UNITED STATES AND JAPANESE
MULTINATIONAL ENTERPRISES

	Subsidiary's influence (A)	Headquarter's influence (B)	Difference (A − B)
Swedish MNEs (24 subsidiaries)	4.10	2.49	1.61
United States MNEs (21 subsidiaries) ...	3.39	2.72	0.67
Japanese MNEs (31 subsidiaries)	3.93	2.18	1.75

Source: Hedlund, 1981.
Note: Measured on a scale from 1 (centralised) to 5 (decentralised) columns A and B indicate the average level of centralisation/decentralisation for each group of multinational enterprises over the range of decisions investigated. The difference between the values of A and B (i.e., A − B) shows whether the influence of the parent (negative value) or the subsidiary (positive value) dominates over the range of decisions investigated.

headquarter's influence also differs, the difference of both values of influence (i.e. between parent influence and subsidiary influence) should also be examined. This difference shows that the influence of subsidiaries dominates that of the headquarters in each country sample. The distribution of influence between subsidiary and headquarters in Swedish and Japanese multinational enterprises is quite similar while United States multinationals seem to have the least difference.

Some more details of the relative influence of the subsidiary in decision making are found in the study of Negandi and Welge[38]. Tables 9 and 10 reveal some differences between United States, Japanese and German multinational enterprises. For all items, United States headquarters seem to grant their foreign affiliates less autonomy on average than their Japanese and German counterparts. The autonomy of the subsidiaries of Japanese multinational enterprises seems to be higher than that of German subsidiaries for all decisions except two, both of which concern production decisions. As seen from Table 10, the influence of the subsidiary is greater than that of the headquarters for the substantial majority of items. In this respect there is no major difference between the multinational enterprises of the three countries investigated. The study by Brand and Hulbert[39], who investigated explicitly the relationship between nationality of parent and extent of headquarters guidance in the marketing function, also found no significant relationship.

A number of studies have examined possible differences in approaches to decision making related to the nationality of the parent firm, where generally United States companies are compared with European or Japanese companies. Ergas and Reid[40] for example, noted that European multinationals often display a "mother-daughter" relationship, with relatively loose ties, although such ties are generally implemented at the most senior level. By comparison, United States companies, which often had considerable experience in organising and coordinating various home activities tended to apply home patterns internationally and adopt integrated worldwide structures for their foreign operations. Young, Hood and Hamill's study of foreign subsidiaries in the United Kingdom[41] also noted that subsidiaries of United States companies are subject to higher levels of control than their European counterparts, the difference being especially marked in the case of financial decisions. In

Table 9. THE RELATIVE INFLUENCE OF THE SUBSIDIARY IN DECISION MAKING

Raw score

Item	Mean scores		
	United States MNEs	Japanese MNEs	German MNEs
Personnel training programme for your subsidiary	3.8	4.6	4.5
Layoffs of operating personnel	4.4	4.9	4.4
Use of expatriate personnel from headquarters.................	2.7	3.6	2.4
Appointment of chief executive of your subsidiary	1.5	2.8	1.7
Maintenance of production facilities at your subsidiary	3.3	4.3	4.8
Determining aggregate production schedule....................	3.2	4.2	4.3
Expansion of your production capacity	2.5	3.5	2.7
Use of local advertising agency	3.9	4.7	4.5
Servicing of products sold...................................	4.4	4.7	4.7
Pricing of products sold in your local market	3.0	4.5	4.0
Introduction of a new product in your local market	2.6	4.1	3.1
Choice of public accountant	2.7	4.6	4.4
Extension of credit to one of your major customers	3.7	4.5	4.3
Use of cash flow in your subsidiary	3.2	4.2	3.4
Your borrowing from local banks or financial institutions	3.2	3.6	3.4
Average...	3.21	4.19	3.77

Source: Negandhi and Welge, 1984.
Note: The responses were pre-coded from "1" for "very little or no influence of the subsidiary" to "5" for "very high influence of the subsidiary".

Table 10. RELATIVE INFLUENCE OVER 15 DECISION AREAS

Mean score differences

Item	Differences in means		
	United States MNEs	Japanese MNEs	German MNEs
Personnel training	1.1	3.1	2.4
Layoffs	2.6	3.3	2.7
Expatriates	−0.7	0.2	−1.7
Appointment of CEO	−3.0	−1.6	−3.0
Maintenance	0.1	1.8	2.4
Production schedule	−0.1	1.2	1.9
Expansion	−1.4	−0.2	−1.2
Advertising	1.4	2.7	2.7
Servicing	2.5	2.9	3.1
Pricing	−0.5	1.9	1.3
New products	−1.2	0.8	−0.6
Choice of CPA	−0.5	1.8	2.4
Credit of customers	1.2	2.4	2.5
Use of cash flow	0.1	1.7	0.3
Borrowing from banks	0.1	0.5	0.1
Average (means)	0.11	1.50	1.02

Source: Negandhi and Welge, 1984.
Note: The figures in the Table represent the differences in means between the subsidiary's and the headquarter's influence for each of the decision items and the means taken over for the companies in the identified country category. A positive number implies a relatively greater influence on the part of the subsidiary, while a negative number indicates greater influence by the headquarters.

contrast, Van Den Bulke and Halsberghe's study on Belgium[42] found that financial control was generally stricter in European than in United States subsidiaries; Dutch and German subsidiaries were found to have very little say, although British and French ones appeared to be more independent than their United States counterparts.

While Dunning's study for the United Kingdom[43] compares present patterns in Japanese subsidiaries with those found in United States subsidiaries nearly 30 years ago, it still provides some interesting insights on Japanese companies, which appear to exercise strong influence over the activities of their United Kingdom subsidiaries. While account is taken of particular features relating to Japanese direct investment in the United Kingdom, such as it being relatively recent, particular ownership patterns and cultural and linguistic aspects, Dunning associated high levels of control with the more holistic approach to decision making in Japanese companies where the importance of features such as the right work ethic, group consciousness and team support require cohesive, integrated decision making policies and centralised control and monitoring. While there is prima facie loose control with respect to salaries and industrial relations, personnel policies concerning recruitment, standards, discipline and wages and incentives aim to ensure consistency with overall business philosophy, particularly the production of high quality, reliable goods at competitive prices. As a result of the latter, little leeway for autonomy was found in areas such as product policy, production control, budgetary planning and costing.

In interpreting some of the patterns reported above, Egelhoff[44] found that United States multinational enterprises tend to exercise relatively high levels of output control over their foreign subsidiaries, whereas European multinational enterprises tend to exercise relatively high levels of behaviour control; in other words, the affiliates of United States multinational enterprises submit more performance data to the parent headquarters than do subsidiaries of European multinationals while the latter tend to fill a significantly higher percentage of key marketing and manufacturing positions in foreign countries with parent company nationals than do United States or United Kingdom multinationals. Similar finds are reported by Brandt and Hulbert[45].

Taking into account that the list of items in the above-noted study by Hedlund contains more – to say it in Egelhoff's terms – output control variables than behavioural control variables, it seems that the observed differences in autonomy are not so much a matter of level but rather of the kinds of instruments used to ensure a specific level of autonomy. That behavioural control can be a sound, but subtle means for achieving accordance of decision making with superior goals is well known since Ouchi's[46] "Theory Z". Behavioural control through the staffing of key positions with parent company nationals has much to do with autonomy, because the home country manager – the expatriate – will act and make decisions in accordance with the parent company, as he is influenced by a lengthy and continuing process of socialisation and acculaturisation in the parent organisation. In this sense, a real autonomy may not exist as such a manager is attuned to the philosophy of the parent and his decisions will likely be in favour of the parent organisation rather than the host country in situations of conflicting goals and pressures.

– *Size*

One of the most frequently examined contextual factors is the size of the company. Despite, or perhaps because, numerous empirical studies have dealt with it, the findings are not very consistent. For example, Brandt and Hulbert found no significant relationship between the size of the parent and the extent of headquarter guidance in marketing. Similarly, Cray[47] did not detect a significant influence of parent size, measured in terms of the number of employees, on the degree of headquarters control of United States multinational enterprises over their subsidiaries in France and England. In contrast, Picard[48] found in his sample of 56 United States-based subsidiaries of foreign multinational enterprises a direct relationship between the size of the total corporation and the autonomy for decisions regarding pricing, advertising and sales promotion, new products, brand names and product line and other marketing decisions, such that the larger the total enterprise, the more autonomy was granted to the United States subsidiaries. A similar conclusion was found by Yunker[49] in her study of 52 multinational enterprises listed in Fortune 500, where overall autonomy increased with the size of the whole company (measured in terms of world sales).

The inverse relationship was reported by Abell[50], as seen from Table 11, which indicates a negative association between the size of the parent and limits on capital expenditure. In other words, the larger the parent the more tightly it controls its subsidiaries with respect to financial matters. The theoretical rationale used to support his finding is that a close connection across frontiers is clearly expensive and the small company does not have the resources to do so. In companies which do have the resources, on the other hand, this very fact may be an extra pressure for a close relationship. Some of these resources, in the form of functional staff at head office, will be an active pressure group advocating a closer arrangement. As suggested by Brooke and Remmers[51], the large company establishes a closer relationship because it can afford it.

In comparison, the empirical study of Kenter[52] revealed no indication of a statistically significant relationship between the size of the total corporation and the planned, ideal

Table 11. CAPITAL EXPENDITURE LIMIT
AND SIZE OF PARENT

Maximum capital expenditure (£ 000)	Percentage distribution of enterprises	
	"Small" parent	"Large" parent
0-2	39.1	44.2
2-4	6.3	9.3
4-6	5.8	11.6
6-8	—	2.3
8-10	0.9	0.8
10-12	3.2	7.8
12-14	0.5	0.8
15-19	0.5	0.8
20+	28.7	16.3
No answers	15.3	6.2
	100.0	100.0

Source: Abell, 1974.
Note: Of particular interest in this table is not so much the levels of capital expenditure limits which have obviously changed since the time of the study but rather the comparisons between large and small parents with respect to the setting of such limits.

autonomy level to be reached by the headquarters of 22 large German multinational enterprises. However, this study did detect some relationships between the intensity of various control instruments used by headquarters to reach the degree of autonomy perceived as ideal. These findings seem to support the argument that control intensity varies directly with the size of the total company for the finance, investment and marketing areas, with the opposite being true for the personnel area.

Again, this hints to the fact that overall autonomy is a rather crude measure and that autonomy should be examined for various areas independently. Judging from the findings presented here, it can be inferred that the delegation of decision-making authority varies to some extent with the size of the corporation. For critical, strategic-type decisions, headquarters may try to reach a relatively high degree of control, and use the capacities of the parent company, especially in marketing and finance, while in decision areas characterised more as operative (e.g. personnel, perhaps with the exception of the appointment of the chief executive officer) they tend to exercise less control with growing size.

– *Degree of internationalisation*

When the degree of internationalisation of a multinational corporation is measured, the number of foreign countries in which the multinational enterprise has subsidiaries is often used. The relationship of this indicator with subsidiary autonomy is again not very clear according to the findings in several studies, as indicated in Table 12.

An important point nonetheless is that it is in those studies which dealt with autonomy in respect of marketing and related functions that the two positive correlations can be observed, i.e. that autonomy in marketing decisions is high when the degree of internationalisation is high and is expected to be low when subsidiaries exist only in a few foreign countries. To some

Table 12. RELATIONSHIP BETWEEN DIFFERENT KINDS OF AUTONOMY
AND DEGREE OF INTERNATIONALISATION IN VARIOUS EMPIRICAL STUDIES

Author	Direction of relationship	Decision areas investigated	Sample characteristics
Cray, 1984	Negative	All	57 subs of 34 US MNEs
Yunker, 1983	Positive	Internal (marketing, selling and purchasing)	52 subs from Fortune 500
Brandt/Hulbert, 1977	Curvilinear	Marketing	63 Brazilian subs of US European and Japanese MNEs
Picard, 1979	Positive	Marketing	56 US-based subs of foreign MNEs
Youssef, 1975	Negative	All	302 US MNEs
Abell, 1974	Negative	Finance	n.a.

Note: For the decision area(s) investigated, the table notes the nature of the relationship between subsidiary autonomy and degree of internationalisation of the group. A positive relationship means that subsidiary autonomy in the decision area investigated increases with the degree of internationalisation of the group and a negative relationship means that autonomy decreases as internationalisation increases. A curvilinear relationship (in the case in question) means that up to a certain degree of internationalisation subsidiary autonomy is lower, and thereafter higher.

extent, the Brandt and Hulbert study supports this insofar as the curvilinear relationship found in their study indicates that multinational enterprises with a high degree of internationalisation grant a higher degree of autonomy to their subsidiaries than those with subsidiaries in a moderate number of foreign countries.

The reason for these positive correlations might be that as the variability of the environment increases with the total number of countries in which a multinational enterprise is operating, marketing decisions require fast reactions based on detailed local knowledge and that the headquarters "far-away back home" would therefore be overcharged with these requirements. In this sense, therefore, headquarters is "forced" to give a considerably higher amount of decision-making authority to operating units.

However, as the synergy potential which characterises multinational enterprises has to be ensured, it is understandable that for compensation purposes the highly internationalised firm will exert a higher amount of control over subsidiaries with respect to finance than ones which are not. The total degree of autonomy then could be negative compared with multinational enterprises present in just a few countries, thus explaining the negative relationship found between the degree of internationalisation and the autonomy level in finance as well as for overall autonomy.

– *Corporate strategy*

Another important parent company factor in the explanation of planned autonomy levels concerns aspects of their corporate strategy. In the study of Kenter, all of those multinational enterprises examined which pursued a growth strategy planned to grant a high level of autonomy in personnel decisions to their foreign subsidiaries. It was also found that enterprises with this overall strategy planned to grant a significantly higher autonomy level than those with a retrenchment or turnaround strategy. In order to explain these findings it can be assumed that where a growth strategy is pursued, the marketing and selling functions become crucial. In order to be successful in this respect, personnel are needed with high knowledge of local market conditions. As these people, however, can only be recruited by the local subsidiaries, a high level of autonomy is needed. In the cases of retrenchment and turnaround strategies, other functions become critical, such as planning and controlling. These, however, are functions which are standardised on a company-wide basis and where autonomy is therefore lower. Also, with respect to decisions concerning disinvestment, Ghertman[53] found that parents tended to make the crucial decisions without consulting the subsidiary, although he notes that this often conceals successive attempts to improve the viability of the subsidiary.

Also, multinational enterprises which follow a recognisable and explicit corporate strategy perceive a level of autonomy which is the highest of all multinational enterprises. This may be explained in that an explicit and world-wide, well-known corporate strategy contains many control effects which enable managers all over the world to make decisions and act in accordance with the superior corporate objectives of the multinational enterprises. Accordingly, the parent enterprise will be willing to grant a higher degree of autonomy.

b) *Parent-subsidiary links*

The literature suggests that there are some factors related to the linkages or ties between parent companies and their subsidiaries which may have an influence on the division of decision making authority. Two broad sets of factors can be discussed in this context – first, the nature by which the foreign subsidiary is established and the degree of parent ownership and, secondly, the degree of interdependence between parent and subsidiary.

– *Establishment and ownership*

As recalled in chapter I, there are many different forms of international involvement. Full or majority owned subsidiaries, greenfield investments, joint ventures, acquisitions, mergers, licencing and partnerships of various sorts represent some of the main forms.

Most of the empirical studies looking at the influence of ownership suggests that as parent ownership increases, the degree of autonomy in decision making in subsidiaries decreases, for the simple reason that holding the majority of the subsidiary's equity enables the parent to exercise the level of control it wishes. Decisions concerning the commitment of major capital resources are among those where the parent company is most likely to retain final authority, at least in respect of wholly or majority owned subsidiaries, particularly when they concern matters of such importance that success or failure would have a material effect on the performance of the enterprise as a whole. This retention of final authority is required by the responsibility and accountability of management to shareholders for the profitability of all the assets of the enterprise.

In an examination of decision making in wholly owned subsidiaries and international joint ventures, Zeira and Shenkar[54] found that wholly owned subsidiaries were generally under stricter parental control particularly for financial issues. They explain this by the view that if the subsidiary fails, one company assumes the total damage whereas in joint ventures damage is limited to each partner's share. It was also suggested that joint ventures may have greater leeway for manoeuvre between two or more parents in decision making because of the larger number of actors involved as well as arising from their greater national and organisational diversity.

The above conclusions rest on the assumption that the joint venture approach is the one ideally preferred in the case in question. However, to the extent that a parent may prefer to invest via a wholly-owned subsidiary but in fact goes ahead instead with a joint venture (which may arise, for example, because of the host country's investment regime) this may affect the willingness of a parent, even when it has majority control in the joint venture, to delegate authority. In such a situation, the company may wish to ensure as much control as possible, for example via the provision of technology or information, ensuing a majority on the board of the joint venture or in having its own people in key positions.

Table 13. METHOD OF ESTABLISHMENT OF FOREIGN COMPANIES
AND LOCUS OF DECISION-MAKING [1]

Decisions	Percentage of subsidiaries with a decisive headquarters influence			
	Joint ventures n = 20	Take-overs n = 33	New estab-lishments n = 94	Others [2] n = 5
Financial decisions				
1. Setting of financial targets	25	30	54	60
2. Preparation of yearly budget	5	3	24	20
3. Acquisition of funds for working capital	40	27	40	40
4. Choice of capital investment projects	30	9	33	40
5. Financing of investment projects	45	30	39	40
6. Target rate of return on investment	60	51	61	80
7. Sale of fixed assets	40	12	27	20
8. Dividend policy	85	82	79	60
9. Royalty payments to parent company	85	76	76	80
Production/marketing decisions				
10. Output volume	15	3	21	—
11. Product range	25	18	25	—
12. Introduction of new products	35	18	31	20
13. Withdrawal of products	25	21	25	20
14. Markets supplied by United Kingdom subsidiary	50	30	43	60
15. Entering new United Kingdom markets	15	12	15	20
16. Entering new non-United Kingdom markets	60	39	47	40
17. Price policy	15	9	12	20
18. Advertising and sales promotion	10	—	5	—
19. Distribution	5	6	9	20
Employment/personnel decisions				
20. Union recognition	—	3	4	—
21. Collective bargaining	—	—	1	—
22. Wage increases	5	3	7	—
23. Numbers employed	10	3	12	20
24. Lay-offs/redundancies	5	3	10	20
25. Hiring of workers	15	3	9	20
26. Recruitment of executives	20	6	15	20
27. Recruitment of senior managers	10	6	12	20
Other decisions				
28. R&D	55	36	48	60
29. Technology employed	50	27	36	60

Source: Young, Hood and Hamill, 1985.
Note: 1. Based on a sample of 152 foreign subsidiaries.
  2. Five firms which were established in the United Kingdom through the acquisition of another previously foreign-owned company.
  n. Sample size.

A number of interesting differences in the degree of decision making centralisation in relation to the method of establishment were found in the study by Young, Hood and Hamill[55] the results of which are summarised in table 13. As expected, subsidiaries established through the take-over of a United Kingdom company were less centrally controlled then was the case for greenfield establishments. This was the case for most of the decision areas examined, but especially so for most financial decisions and production and marketing decisions concerning output volume, introduction of new products and markets supplied. However, in the case of the acquisition of another previously foreign-owned company, the change in parent appeared to be associated with a shift to more central control, with poor performance prior to the acquisition explaining this shift.

– *Interdependence in the international network*

Interdependence between the component parts of a multinational enterprise, often measured in terms of intra-company flows of goods and services, is felt by many researchers to have a very important influence on decision making patterns. The following descussion of the role of interdependence examines this topic first of all from the perspective of the parent company and subsequently from that of the subsidiary.

In considering the degree of interdependence of the international network as a contextual factor of the autonomy level, a useful approach, following a suggestion of Kenter[56], is to examine the general level of autonomy the parent company would ideally wish to grant to its foreign subsidiaries. This seems to be the most appropriate way of examining the relationship between a parent-specific contextual factor and the theoretical construction of autonomy, because it is clear that there may be a difference between the planned, ideal level of decision-making delegation and the authority level in reality. In the study of Brooke and Remmers[57], for example, it was discovered that there was often a substantial difference between the intention of the head office and the result at subsidiary level.

In Kenter's study, the interdependence between the component parts of multinational enterprises, turned out to be one of the most – perhaps the most – important factor in explaining whether a high or low level of planned autonomy can be expected. The causal analysis led to the conclusion that the planned autonomy level (which is the one the headquarters wanted to achieve) for finance and investment decisions was higher the more goods and services are transferred from the parent company to all the foreign subsidiaries. An explanation for this relatively strong relationship could be that in a multinational enterprise in which a great deal of raw materials and semi-finished goods are delivered from the parent to the affiliates, the subsidiaries are most likely to be assembling affiliates. In such cases major (expansion) investments are likely to occur only very seldom. On the other hand, headquarters perceived an ideal autonomy level for marketing decisions which was lower the closer were the interdependencies. The dependence of the parent company on its affiliates was very high especially in the marketing area, and it is expected to be higher the more it must rely on the marketing and selling expertise of the affiliate. In the view of Garnier[58] dependence is the most important element in the determination of autonomy, particularly the parent company's dependence on its affiliate or the interdependece between the two organisations.

From the perspective of the subsidiary, Kenter also noted that it is important to know whether the foreign subsidiary delivers goods to the parent company or whether there exists an inverse flow of goods and services. Furthermore, the flow of goods and services between a specific foreign affiliate and its sister companies in the same concern should also be considered and, again, this flow can be bidirectional. Table 14 shows the correlation coefficients of these

Table 14. RELATIONSHIPS BETWEEN DIFFERENT FORMS OF INTERDEPENDENCE AND AUTONOMY LEVEL IN THREE FUNCTIONAL AREAS

Autonomy levels in various decision areas	Nature of interdependence			
	Flow from single sub to other subs	Flow from other subs to single sub	Flow bottom-up	Flow top-down
Investment and finance	− 0.6233	+ 0.7169	− 0.3090	− 0.6903
Personnel		+ 0.3428		
Marketing.........................	+ 0.4352		+ 0.7572	+ 0.3894

Source: Kenter, 1985.

Note: The table reports on how autonomy levels in various decision areas (e.g., investment and finance) vary with respect to the form of interdependence in the international network, as proxied by different directions of flows of goods and services between the subsidiary and other parts of the multinational enterprise.

four dimensions of interdependence with the realised level of autonomy in the functional areas of investment and finance, personnel and marketing.

From this it can be inferred that the autonomy level for investment and finance decisions is significantly influenced by all four dimensions of interdependence. Detailed inspection reveals that the autonomy level is lower in this area the more the parent company is involved. The more the parent company – regarded from the subsidiary perspective – receives goods and services and the more it delivers to a single subsidiary, the more are investment and finance decisions concentrated at the headquarter level. Garnier (1982) detected the same negative relationship for the overall autonomy of the subsidiary, while Welge[59] found that the dependence of a subsidiary on the parent company was the most important factor influencing the degree of decision-making authority of a foreign subsidiary. Moreover, the more the subsidiary delivers to its sister subsidiaries the lower is its autonomy.

The findings of the studies mentioned above all point in the same direction and support the idea that decision-making authority is lower the greater is the importance of a subsidiary for the parent company and the whole corporation. These empirical results and interpretations are also in accordance with the findings of Hedlund[60] who did not differentiate between whether a subsidiary receives or delivers material and immaterial goods to or from the parent company, but rather examined of the degree of interdependence between units in general.

On the other hand, Table 14 also shows that a high level of autonomy can be expected in the investment and finance areas when the foreign affiliate receives a relatively high amount of goods and services from other subsidiaries of the same concern. This finding also holds true for the personnel area. In this respect, the subsidiary finds itself in a situation where involvement with the parent company is not very intensive and where the direct importance of the subsidiary's activities for the parent is not very great.

While the degree of autonomy in investment and finance decisions tends to become lower as the importance of the subsidiary for the parent company increases, it tends to become higher in the marketing area, a similar result also being reported by Picard[61]. This finding is explained in that the more a subsidiary delivers to sister units and/or to the parent company, the less important is the marketing function for this subsidiary and, accordingly, the more decision-making authority can be granted and is granted in reality. In this interpretation it should also be borne in mind that the internal norms of the goods delivered top-down exert a considerable amount of control, especially in the marketing area.

c) *Characteristics specific to subsidiaries*

– *Country of location*

A number of authors have investigated the question of whether the country of location of the subsidiary can be expected to have an influence on the degree of subsidiary autonomy. In this respect, it might be argued that the higher the host country risk, the lower should be the degree of autonomy granted to the subsidiary. This hypothesis, however, could not be supported by the few empirical studies on the subject; indeed, the opposite seems to hold true. Cray[62] as well as Garnier[63] found that subsidiaries located in France are less autonomous than subsidiaries in other countries such as Mexico (Garnier) and England (Cray), a finding that is quite unexpected in the sense that the French environment is relatively stable and predicatable. Bearing in mind that both of the studies referred to are based on samples of firms with United States parents, Cray noted that while it would be tempting to attribute the above-noted difference to language difficulties or other problems of communication, which would prompt United States managers to impose more direct control over French subsidiaries, there was no evidence to support this explanation. Rather, Cray felt that it is probably more useful to look at the United States manager's perception of France as a business environment for an explanation of these results and in this context noted that while the direct effects of government policy on multinational corporations have not been noticably different in France than in the United Kingdom, previous nationalisations had raised questions about government attitude towards large foreign-owned businesses at the time of his enquiry. This probably did not translate directly into a perceived need for more control but contributed to a general uneasiness that is shown up in efforts to maintain greater predictability through direct control.

If this explanation is valid, it could be expected that multinational enterprises also take these considerations into account. That seems not to be the case, at least for German enterprises, in that Welge's[64] findings suggest that there is no substantial difference in the autonomy level which German parent companies are willing to grant to subsidiaries in countries as different as France, India and the United States.

– *Size*

As was the case for company-wide characteristics, one of the most often examined contextual factors is the size of the foreign subsidiary. Similarly, the pattern of influence is not homogeneous. Out of eleven studies which examined this relationship, seven could not support the hypothesis of Alsegg[65] of the importance of the subidiary size for the level of autonomy. The remaining four studies revealed contradictory findings. Cray[66] and Egelhoff[67] detected a negative relationship between autonomy and size, whereas Picard[68] and Hedlund[69] report a positive and significant correlation.

In interpreting these conflicting findings, Hedlund has noted that, from a theoretical standpoint, two conflicting forces can be detected. On the one hand, increased size means that the subsidiary can build up its own resources, have its own specialists and become less dependent on central management or, to the extent that size reflects success, this can enhance the voice of the subsidiary in corporate decisions. On the other hand, a very large subsidiary is of great importance to the whole company, and may therefore require the attention of the parent. Indeed, close inspection of the data reveals a tendency towards a curvilinear relationship, i.e. as size increases, so too does the autonomy level, up to some point, whereafter autonomy begins to fall. Hedlund found that this relationship is not significantly affected by the influence of third variables such as product flows, technology transfer or market share and profitability of the subsidiary.

– Performance

The performance of a foreign affiliate is another factor that has been evaluated with respect to possible influence on autonomy levels. In general it might be assumed that poor performance would attract greater parent attention, but equally good performance, particularly for a large subsidiary, might do likewise if the subsidiary represents an important position in the overall affairs of the enterprise. These possible differences in the role that performance may play are reflected in the results of studies where some have found a positive relationship (e.g. Picard), others a negative one (e.g. Garnier) or a non-significant one (e.g. Hedlund, Cray). These differences in results suggest, therefore, that subsidiary performance does not have a clear, single or even significant influence on autonomy levels.

– Age

A positive correlation between the age of a subsidiary and the degree of autonomy was found by researchers such as Youssef[70] and Picard[71], suggesting that foreign subsidiaries may enjoy a greater amount of autonomy when they are older and are no longer in the stage of establishing. It has also been argued that the relationship between the age of subsidiaries and their degree of autonomy often tends to be more complex, with close supervision from the parent company when the subsidiary is starting its activities, or at a much later stage when the subsidiary's markets tend to stagnate or decline, with greater autonomy for the subsidiary in between these two extreme stages.

d) *Summary and Archetypes with respect to the situation of subsidiaries*

On the basis of the empirical evidence reported in this section, it may be possible to define some archetypes of subsidiaries where a higher/lower degree of autonomy may be expected.

On this basis, a foreign subsidiary may be seen as having relatively little autonomy if it belongs to a large multinational group established in many foreign countries; if it manufactures fairly standardised products; if the activities of the members are largely integrated, with important interflows of products between them (this holds true especially for the investment and finance function); if it has been created to serve a market larger than the country in which it is established; or if the parent company holds a large portion of its equity. On the other hand, a subsidiary may be seen as more autonomous if it was acquired to serve mainly the local market; if it belongs to a small group; if it has interchange of products with the rest of the group and is operating in an activity slightly different from that of the other members (the opposite holds true for the marketing function); if an important part of its common shares is held by local investors; and if the whole concern pursues a growth strategy.

Another way of summarising the pressures towards centralisation and decentralisation has been given by Brooke and Black[72] whose findings are condensed in Table 15. Of particular note here is that the same factor can have either a positive or a negative impact on subsidiary autonomy. Obviously, there is no safe basis on which to say that contextual and environmental variables are highly correlated with autonomy. Most of the variables leave a considerable degree of freedom to corporate management with respect to how to design effectively the relationship with their foreign susbsidiaries – in other words, an important degree of strategic choice appears to be involved.

Table 15. SOME FACTORS AFFECTING CENTRALISATION AND DECENTRALISATION

Factors	Relationship with centralisation	Relationship with decentralisation
Size of subsidiary	A large subsidiary could influence the results of the group too much to be left alone, and there would therefore be a tendency to control it	A large subsidiary may have the know-how to operate comparatively independently, and therefore tend to operate on a decentralised basis
Use of expatriate staff	Use of expatriate staff could be interpreted as a sign of centralisation	Expatriate staff could be seen as sufficiently competent to run the subsidiary independently
Finance	Centralised financial planning makes the formulation of a global strategy easier	
Economic instability	A tight hold of the reins is indicated because of the risk involved	Greater use of local sources of finance minimises exchange losses
Communications	Long lines of communication with head office, standardised reporting, and flow of information are necessary for worldwide operations	Expense of supporting centralised reporting system can be too great, especially for small companies
Technology	A sophisticated technology, especially if "politically sensitive", is often retained in home country	"Ear to the ground" in subsidiary is needed to take advantage of new developments

Source: Brooke and Black, 1976.
Note: The table indicates how some selected factors may be associated with a centralised or decentralised approach to decision making.

2. External factors

a) *Economic and social conditions*

To an important extent, the manner in which an enterprise organises its activities depends on the economic situation, and as the latter changes so too can changes in organisational structure be expected. The major and structural changes in the economic situation that have been continuing since the early 1970s with respect to, for example, growth, stability, uncertainty, competition and so on have been well documented[73]. The intention of this section is therefore to examine how particular features of these changes affect organisational structure.

Recession and slow growth, leading to significant unemployment and important changes in the demand for various skills, have affected most nations and many industries since the mid-seventies and resulted in major pressures for structural adjustment. Growth opportunities have become much more limited and while there has recently been some improvement in the economic outlook, this has not spread equally to all countries or industries. There has been an important upsurge in the competitive environment. In part, this has resulted from the movement of resources from saturated or declining markets to expanding ones and in part due to the emergence of new entrants particularly on the international scene, such as new ventures by state-owned enterprises or enterprises from the Newly Industrialising Countries, while other firms have expanded into the international arena as a response to adjustment pressures. A particular aspect of greater competitive pressures has been the reemergence of the importance of price competition such that business has generally become much more cost conscious.

These changes have also been associated with increased levels of uncertainty and instability. Substantial and often abrupt swings in exchange rates and interest rates, and the important differences in these between countries has also made enterprises more sensitive to the cost of their funds and the return on liquid assets at any one particular time or place. Similarly, there have been important changes in demand patterns, which have also been unpredictable in some cases. An interesting development here has been the growing similarity in tastes for certain goods worldwide, despite national and cultural differences and this has been seen as both cause and effect of the growing internationalisation of markets.

Indeed, an important feature of the present economic situation has been the increasing internationalisation of the world economy, which has caused many multinational enterprises, particularly the larger ones to see their operations in a global perspective. The need to keep costs as low as possible and to recoup the often vast expenditures on technology in modern production facilities has meant, for many enterprises, that production levels have to attain a given size to achieve economies of scale, yet the resultant scale of production can be such that discrete markets, even in individual major economies are no longer large enough and world or at least regional markets are necessary to sell the resulting output. In some cases, the required investment, technology and output are such that even large multinational enterpriese may find it necessary or desireable to organise production and distribution by joint ventures or other arrangements with other large or multinational enterprises.

The combination of cost pressures and global markets has important implications for multinational enterprises operating at this scale. First of all, operation at a global scale provides considerable opportunities to achieve important savings, for example in locating production units in lowest cost locations or in purchasing inputs from lowest cost sources. However, at any point in the system delays, inefficiencies and bottlenecks may be costly, requiring therefore coordination of production and distribution to minimise inventories and maximise the speed with which the production process can be adapted to changes in demand. This may often require the centralisation of particular functions in order to achieve economies of scale, for example in marketing, by gathering and making available centrally market research information, in distribution by centralised scheduling, in R&D by sharing scarce and expensive resources and avoiding duplication of effort, in purchasing, by buying inputs centrally at bulk rates, and in financial management where fluctuating exchange and interest rates must be monitered and directed at the central level to reduce exposure or exploit opportunities arising from rate differentials.

The above imply important pressures on multinational enterprises to seek greater internal integration of their operations. At the level of manufacturing, for example, closer integration of the activities of plants in different countries may be essential to increasing plant level economies of scale, while consolidation of responsibility at worldwide or regional product divisions may be necessary to integrate an often diverse range of facilities. Equally, integration of global financial management has been considered necessary to hedge against exchange and interest rate risk, while coordinated R&D, product engineering and manufacturing strategies can exploit technological advantages and increase technological competitiveness by reducing the lag between innovation and development and by strengthening feedback.

A second important implication of the above is the growing need for flexibility at the level of individual subsidiaries to react to changes in the local market or production area. In an often rapidly changing and unpredictable environment, cost and risk reduction assume increasing importance and flexibility must be maintained if the enterprise is to predict, identify and react to changes as quickly as possible. A major concern of multinational enterprises is therefore that of reconciling often opposing pressures for integration and operational flexibility, and this requires improved coordination. It is in this context that it is appropriate at this stage to discuss the role of new technology, specifically information technology, which is often viewed as playing an important role in the way in which large and complex multinational enterprises organise their operations.

b) *Competition*

The changes in economic conditions noted above have had an important impact on market structures and the modalities of competition between enterprises. These in turn may affect the way in which enterprises, particularly multinational enterprises organise their activities. For example, in many cases, multinational enterprises are more often confronted with the same competitors in many markets or in global markets whereas, previously, competition between any two given enterprises in many instances tended to be limited to a few local markets. In other cases, and sometimes with a view to increasing market share in global markets, enterprises may cooperate with others directly, or by developing linkages with other enterprises in individual national markets in order to gain economies in areas such as production, marketing or R & D. Such cooperation, often found in the past in primary sector activities is now evident in some manufacturing and service sector activities. As a result, multinational enterprises are more often faced with pressures tending to modify their global organisational structure in order to remain efficient with respect to their competitors, who may already have gone through a rationalisation process in this respect, or in order to maintain competitive when operating in global markets.

Pressures from competitors also require enterprises to react more rapidly to changes in the situation of their market, which may have consequences for the way in which enterprises are organised. Also, the fact that competition between multinational enterprises takes place more often now in many markets simultaneously or in global markets tends to erode more rapidly the particular advantages that a multinational enterprise may possess at any particular point in time. As a consequence, more frequent changes in strategy may be required to maintain such competitive advantages. This again may affect the ways in which enterprises organise their activities.

c) *Information Technology*

In general, the nature and pace of technological developments have been one of the key sources of structural change and authors such as Dunning[74] have stressed technological developments as one of the most important factors explaining changes in the structure of international production and the operation of multinational enterprises. Technological developments in products and processes can result in opening up new markets or maintaining or increasing established markets as a result of cost changes. Multinational enterprises have generally been strengthening the technological base of their operations, with some proceeding to full product integration along lines of particular technological advantage. Indeed, many of the developments in strategies and with respect to costs, market size, economies of scale and location have been permitted if not determined by technological developments.

A strong technological base not only underlines diversification as a strategic response of multinational enterprise to adjustment pressures, but also forms part of the integration responses of multinational enterprises – indeed, authors such as Doz[75] identify global integration as a major response to improve international competitiveness. As noted above, such responses permit various advantages and economies of scale, but they also result in a greater need for management and integration of activities. It is in this context of the greater need for integration and oversight together with the need to maintain local flexibility, that developments in information technology, and their impact or organisational structure, is discussed.

The organisational requirements of multinational enterprises generally involve information flows and the nature and volume of these flows will be related to the size, complexity, diversity and internationality of operations. This in turn will determine the information requirements with respect to the needs for reporting, monitoring, appraisal, coordination and control. Here, a major feature on modern information technology is that of the volume, speed and reliability of information transmission and it follows that the influence of such technologies on the enterprise will depend on its particular data and information requirements. Thus, where communication flows between parent and subsidiaries are limited, and where time or speed is not an essential factor, there will likely be little cost justification for adopting such technologies. Thus, even some highly multinationalised firms may have only limited needs for modern information technologies. As noted earlier, characteristics specific to a particular industry or the traditional approaches adopted by enterprises from particular home countries to the relationship between parent and subsidiary can have an important bearing.

In discussing the impact of recent developments in information technology on the organisational structures of multinational enterprises, the question is often raised whether this results in increasing parent control over subsidiaries. In addressing this topic, a first point to make is that information technologies can assist multinational enterprises to move to the organisational structure which best fits their requirements, rather than being a force determining the adoption of a particular structure. In reporting on the results of a joint BIAC/OECD survey, Ergas and Reid[76] found that while many companies have been using modern information technologies to help implement a more integrated structure, no cases were found where such a structure was chosen because of the availability of these technologies.

Given its role as a factor facilitating the adoption of particular structures, including perhaps especially integrated structures, any resultant increase in or tendency to centralised control cannot therefore be directly attributed to information technology. This being said, studies[77] have found that decision making authority at the level of the subsidiary is substantially weaker in highly integrated multinational enterprises than in those where there is low interdependence between parent and subsidiary – a predictable conslusion in that higher interdependence requires some mechanism for coordination.

Enterprises adopt a particular structure as a result of the economic and political situation, and having decided on that structure, information technology can play an often important role in supporting that structure. Even when a particular structure facilitated by this technology is associated with a higher degree of centralised control, as has been suggested in the case of integrated structures, the same technology can also be used to maintain or increase subsidiary "voice" and thereby reducing the extent to which a trade-off is involved between coordination and subsidiary autonomy. An OECD study on structural adjustment and multinational enterprises[78] has noted that one of the factors influencing the extent to which coordination and autonomy are compatible rather than mutually exclusive is the extent to which parent and subsidiary objectives are in harmony.

d) *Government policies*

It is well known that government policies can influence international strategies, a typical example being that of tariff barriers which stimulate direct investment to supply the local market as opposed to serving that market via exports. Equally, investment incentives may have an impact on the location, size or nature of the investment, while conditions or performance requirements on inward investments may have certain disincentive effects[79]. Also, and more generally, national regulations and practices in the host country in areas such as labour relations, information provision or decision making involvement, particularly when these differ significantly from those in the home country, may have implications for the subsidiary. In some European countries, for example, there are extensive requirements concerning the provision of information to employees and employee involvement in decision making. This may require particular efforts on behalf of enterprises which are used to adopting certain areas of centralised decision making in the areas concerned which may make it more difficult for the local subsidiary to involve employees in the decision making process. In some instances, it may be that enterprises have to delegate more authority as a result of national legislation in order to continue to meet national requirements in the areas concerned.

The remainder of the section discusses the possible impacts of a number of types of preconditions and performance requirements (which are often typical of but not totally exclusive to host developing countries) on the position of the local subsidiary in the enterprise as a whole.

Typical preconditions and performance requirements often faced by foreign investors, particularly in developing countries, include, inter alia, local content requirements, minimum export levels, local equity participation levels, the employment of host country nationals in key positions, research and development or transfer of technology requirements and international product mandate requirements. The rationales behind such measures, which may sometimes be imposed, in other cases negotiated and to varying extents offset or compensated by investment incentives, may be ideological in nature, for example to increase domestic if not state control, or they may be geared to ensuring or increasing host country benefits. It is sometimes argued that such measures are necessary to counteract particular practices of multinational enterprises which the host country sees as damaging expected benefits from inward direct investment.

The nature or extent of host country demands, as expressed via preconditions and performance requirements, may vary depending, inter alia, on the characteristics of the company, according to the Conference Board Study[80]. For example, it seems that, in comparison to enterprises organised along product lines, those organised along geographic lines tend to experience if not encourage greater demands, to some extent perhaps because they have strategies for dealing with these demands and are more aware of them. Similarly, it can be expected that local demands concerning companies with a high technological base will relate to the transfer of technology or local purchases whereas those geared to companies with a stronger consumer emphasis may face requirements concerning limitations on production levels or local markets. Equally, companies which are more capital intensive may face greater demands than those which are labour intensive, particularly because of the desire to ensure or increase the host country benefits that can accrue from this type of investment

As reported by the companies investigated in the Conference Board study, it was found that, in general, host country demands tend not to be insurmountable. While there are individual examples of companies deciding not to invest or to pull out as a result of these demands, there is normally a degree of give and take between local demands and companies' objectives. However, the extent of this give and take on the part of the enterprise may be constrained by the nature of the host country requirement. For example, in the case of purely business decisions such as purchasing and production, companies appear to be more willing and able to negotiate, such that these types of requirements are not generally seen as having major discouragement effects on the investment or giving rise to organisational changes. However, it is obvious that if such requirements are too onerous, the investment will not go ahead in the first place. To this it might be added that even if the investment were to take place, it may well subsequently fail.

Host country measures concerning local ownership or host country nationals in key positions can sometimes have important effects on the nature of the investment and the decision-making power of the subsidiary, but this depends very much on the situation. For example, requirements concerning local management may be easily met and have no impact on organisational structure if high quality locals are available, with the converse happening if significant differences would exist between local management and parent objectives and philosophies. Requirements concerning local ownership may result in significant losses in corporate authority over capital expenditure decisions, an area where retention of control is most important to many companies. On the other hand, resultant shared risks may mean that the parent is willing to forego some decision making power. In any event, it would seem that, seen in isolation, local ownership may not be a key factor influencing subsidiary autonomy, in part because it appears that the growth of local authority that is associated with local control is often in areas where local say is already substantial.

Local demands for financial control or top management positions can influence the delegation of authority, though in many instances their effect is not decisive, with more traditional considerations such as the status and experience of subsidiary management, the size of the unit, or the length of the period of establishment in the host country often playing a more decisive role. Nevertheless, and depending on the situation of the company and the nature and severity of requirements, local demands may cause the company to limit the structure of the subsidiary such that it meets local requirements but where other activities or functions are provided as needed by the parent. The above discussion on information technology shows how this offers a greater capacity to the enterprise to modify its structure for example, by facilitating limited entry to particular markets with a narrow and specialised activity focus. In turn, this may reduce benefits to the host country, benefits which it had been trying to capture through preconditions and performance requirements.

Chapter IV

DEVELOPMENTS IN ORGANISATIONAL STRUCTURE
OVER TIME

As is clear from the discussion of chapter III above, a wide variety of forces, some internal to the enterprise, others external, influence the choice of appropriate organisational structure. As these forces change over time, and many of them have changed quite dramatically in the last decade or so, it can be expected that these will often be associated with changes in what is felt to be the most suitable organisational structure. It is equally clear from chapter III that these different forces often push for change in different directions and, indeed, the question of appropriate organisational response is often seen as the task of managing competing forces for oversight and flexibility.

While there have certainly been changes in the forces influencing or determining organisational structures, the types of features discussed in chapter I, such as different approaches to international involvement and the role played by intangible forces such as corporate philosophy or personalities, it follows that no one particular trend can be expected as to how multinational enterprises have been modifying their organisational links over time. Clearly then, trends or developments in all directions are to be expected.

This being said, this chapter looks first, at how decision making authority in foreign subsidiaries has been changing over time. There are relatively few studies directly addressing this question and some of these are more qualitative than quantitative in nature. Following this, the chapter takes a more general look at how organisational structures have been developing over time and focuses on some of the main directions identified by researchers and their possible implications for decision making autonomy at the subsidiary level.

1. Empirical studies

Alsegg[81], besides exploring the impact of various contextual factors on subsidiary autonomy, also introduced a conceptually very fruitful extension of the perspective by putting the relation between headquarters and subsidiary and subsidiary effectiveness in a dynamic perspective. It is argued that control intensity will vary according to the developmental stage of the subsidiary; small subsidiaries are more autonomous at the beginning of their development with the necessity to limit local autonomy becoming greater with increasing number and size of subsidiaries. Local managers then enjoy less independence, but their autonomy increases. The manager cannot decide himself on matters of finance and personnel, but he is responsible for a larger business volume.

Alsegg introduced a further dynamic dimension by hypothesising a positive correlation between below-average effectiveness and control intensity. Subsidiaries not meeting the standards of effectiveness will be more strictly controlled in the next planning cycle; above-average subsidiaries, however, will be given more autonomy. Similar to Barlow[82], Alsegg emphasises the dysfunctional consequences of high control intensities in noting that many experts argue that ever stricter controls stifle local initiative and are therefore counterproductive, and that a really capable person will not accept a managerial position when prevented from using the full range of his abilities.

The results of a study by Welge[83] seem to point in the same direction. Decentralisation of headquarter-subsidiary relations is often likely to generate above-average results than high control intensity. In other words, a control strategy allowing for more local autonomy is associated with better effectiveness than a more centralised strategy restricting local autonomy. Autonomous subsidiaries are able to respond more quickly to environmental changes, they are more flexible, and provide able managers with more discretion than those subsidiaries managed centrally by their parent companies. Since selection of foreign managers is regarded as very important, at least by German parent companies, discretion for good managers seems to have an important explanatory power.

Turning to empirical studies which directly address the question of change over time, the study by Young, Hood and Hamill[84] examined changes in parent involvement over the five years preceeding the date of the study. While 38 per cent of the respondents noted no change in parent involvement, 15 per cent felt that the direction of change was significantly more centralised and a further 27 per cent felt this was marginally more so. The main reasons underlying moves towards more central control were felt to be poor performance and moves in the direction of greater global integration, and the authors reported that moves towards rationalisation and restructuring were expected to accelerate this trend.

The Conference Board study[85] found that local authority, regardless of its actual level for different decision areas, had not changed that much over the last decade although there were indications that there was less authority than before concerning decisions to commit capital resources (e.g. establish new plant, acquire existing firms or engage in joint ventures) or to enter new territories. In general, it was found that there was a tendency to greater centralisation in areas where this was already high, with a move towards greater subsidiary autonomy in areas where the subsidiary had already a considerable degree of independence.

In order to assess trends in the development of autonomy over time – and given the lack of empirical material – it is necessary to tackle the problem in an indirect way, initially by examining available studies on organisational structures of multinational enterprises at various points in time, because the structural framework determines to a significant extent subsidiary autonomy.

2. Organisation structures of multinationals

Since the pioneering study of Chandler[86] a large body of empirical research has developed on organisational structures of large, diversified corporations. Chandler's famous hypothesis, "structure follows strategy" has also been dealt with in the context of multinational corporations, by authors such as Brooke and Remmers[87]; Stopford and Wells[88]; Channon[89]; Franko[90]; and Yoshino[91]. From this research, launched under the auspices of the Harvard Multinational Enterprise Project, a theory has been developed known as the evolutionary stages theory of international organisation. According to this theoretical notion, firms initially manage foreign operations through the formation of a separate export unit in the marketing division. As markets grow, the firm becomes involved in foreign licensing

Figure 1

INTERNATIONAL ORGANISATION EVALUATION BY MULTINATIONAL ENTERPRISES

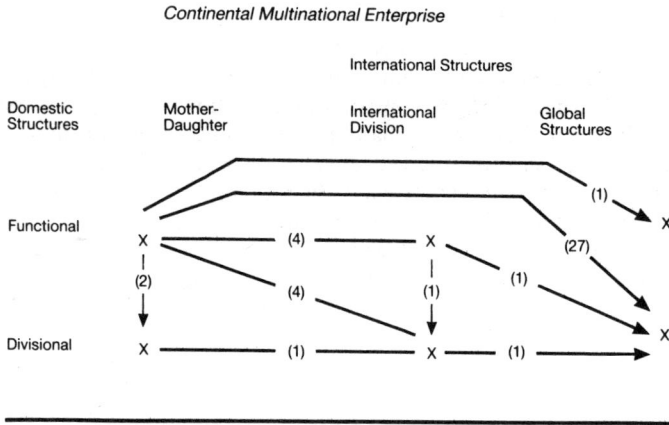

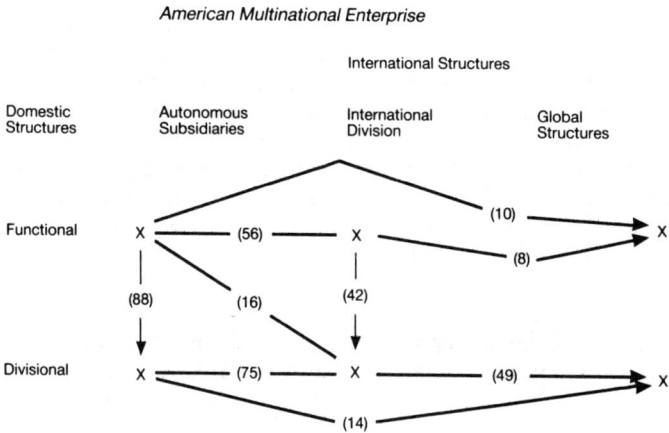

Continental Multinational Enterprise

International Structures

| Domestic Structures | Mother-Daughter | International Division | Global Structures |

Functional X ———— (4) ———— X   (27)   X

(2)   (4)   (1)   (1)   (1)

Divisional X ———— (1) ———— X ——— (1) ———→ X

American Multinational Enterprise

International Structures

| Domestic Structures | Autonomous Subsidiaries | International Division | Global Structures |

Functional X ═══ (56) ═══ X   (10)   X
                                  (8)

(88)   (16)   (42)

Divisional X ═══ (75) ═══ X ——— (49) ———→ X
                           (14)

Source: Franko 1976, p. 203.

Note: The figure shows the paths taken by two groups of multinational enterprises (European and United States) in moving from domestic structures (functional or divisional) to international, global structures. For example, the United States enterprises examined generally began foreign operations with autonomous subsidiaries and the move to global structures (usually associated at some stage with a move from functional to divisional structures) was typically preceeded by a move to international divisional structures. By comparison, the European enterprises examined generally began foreign operations on a mother-daughter basis and generally moved straight to global structures (associated with a change from functional to divisional structures) without going through the intervening international division phase. Figures in parenthesis represent the number of enterprises on a particular path.

Table 16. RELATIONSHIPS BETWEEN ELEMENTS OF CORPORATE STRATEGY
AND TYPES OF ORGANISATIONAL STRUCTURE

Elements of corporate strategy	Types of structure			
	Functional divisions	International divisions	Geographical divisions	Product divisions
Foreign product diversity.............	Low foreign product diversity			High foreign product diversity
Product modification differences between subsidiaries	Low product modification differences between subsidiaries			
Product change				High rate of product change
Size of foreign operations		Relatively small foreign operations	Relatively large foreign operations	Relatively large foreign operations
Size of foreign manufacturing			High level of foreign manufacturing	
Number of foreign subsidiaries	Few foreign subsidiaries	Low to moderate number of foreign subsidiaries	Large number of foreign subsidiaries	Large number of foreign subsidiaries
Extent of outside ownership in foreign subsidiaries	Low level of outside ownership in foreign subsidiaries			
Extent of foreign acquisitions.........	Few foreign acquisitions			

Source: Egelhoff, 1982.
Note: For a given element of corporate strategy, the table shows "typical" approaches adopted in multinational enterprises, depending on their organisational form.

agreements, joint ventures and subsidiaries. The increasing scale of involvement in foreign markets requires new management skills and responsibility for these new international operations is generally placed outside the firm's traditional structure. As foreign operations become more established, most companies create an international division to manage all international operations and as these grow in size and complexity, new organisational pressures and requirements will lead to the adoption of more integrated structures. The main options in this respect have been structures based on functional or product lines, although area, matrix or mixed structures also provide alternative means of organising international operations. According to the evolutionary stages theory of multinational organisation design, firms will progress from an international division to more global structures as the percentage of sales received from foreign operations rises. As Davidson[92] noted, the firm's degree of diversity will play a key role in determining which option is chosen to displace the international division.

Of course, not all enterprises follow exactly the above stylised pattern, and the studies by Stopford and Wells, Franko, and Davidson referred to above report on the international organisational evolution of multinational enterprises. Data on the structural evolution of United States and continental European multinational enterprises are presented in Figure 1, where it can be seen that most of the continental firms simply skipped the international division phase passed through by nearly 90 per cent of the 170 United States multinationals surveyed by Stopford and Wells. Continental moves to the "global" forms of organisation (world-wide product, area, mixed or matrix structures) accompanied divisionalisation by product at home. In contrast, Franko found that more than three-quarters of the United States multinational enterprises examined in his study saw fit to change their domestic structures from functional to divisional forms prior to adopting one of the so-called global structures. Although the evolutionary paths are different in European and United States multinational enterprises, the data indicate a significant trend towards global, integrated structures for both of these groups.

An important question at this point is that of the factors which have put pressure on certain companies to adopt global, integrated structures. One explanatory factor is certainly that the move to a global structure is perceived as a means of integrating international with domestic operations. However, the most important advantage of such structures is the development of a strategic focus. Another explanation is the increasing use of formal portfolio planning systems. As suggested by Davidson, the definition of strategic business units, central to all portfolio planning approaches, tends to promote adoption of a global structure.

It would be too simplistic, however, to argue that all multinationals will move in the direction of global, integrated structures. The extent to which they will adopt global structures depends on various elements of strategy. Table 16 provides some relationships between elements of strategy and types of organisational structure. Another qualification concerning any general trend towards global structures is that there is some evidence in the literature indicating that highly integrated structures, especially three-dimensional matrix structures, are not the final structural archetype. The experience of some large companies show that more simple, specialised, supra-national product management forms are sought, instead of highly complex matrix structures, as suggested by Franko. This seems to be an important structural innovation in order to allow for more local flexibility.

3. Global and multi-local structures

According to the "structure follows strategy" hypothesis, developments towards globally organised structures reflect the growing importance of strategies of rationalisation made necessary by changes in the international economic environment over the past decade. Such strategies involve the integration of production and marketing systems, centralisation of strategic decisions, formalisation of policies and procedures, and tighter control of subsidiaries through financial and other means. The ultimate aim is to achieve economies of scale through greater unification and integration of the various units comprising the enterprise.

According to Porter[93] the sources of global advantage stem from four broad causes: conventional comparative advantage, economies of scale or learning curves extending beyond the scale of cumulative volume achievable in individial national markets, advantages from product differentiation, and the public goods character of market information and technology. These four areas encompass the following advantages: comparative advantage, production economies of scale, global experience, logistical economies of scale, marketing and purchasing economies of scale, product differentiation, proprietary product technology and mobility of production. The sources of global advantage often occur in combination, and there can be interactions among them.

There are also a variety of impediments to realising these advantages of global rationalisation which can block an industry or a firm from becoming global altogether. These impediments can be grouped into three categories: economic, managerial, and institutional. Economic impediments include transportation and storage costs, differing product needs, established distribution channels, sales force, local repair, sensitivity to lead times, complex segmentation within geographic markets and lack of world demand. Managerial impediments include geographically differing marketing tasks, intensive local services, rapidly changing technology, and institutional impediments include government impediments and perceptual or resource impediments.

These impediments are nearly always present to some degree in an industry and in an individual firm. As a result, there may be aspects of "localness" that remain. There are, however, a number of triggers most common in creating global industries. Some of these triggers are created by the environment, others are the result of strategic innovations by the firm. Environmental triggers to globalisation can stem from increased scale economies, decreased transportation or storage costs, rationalised or changed distribution channels, changed factor costs, narrowed national economic and social circumstances and reduced government constraints. Even in the absence of environmental triggers, a firm can begin the process of globalisation by strategic innovations such as product redefinition, identification of market segments, reduced cost of adaptations, design changes, deintegration of production and elimination of constraints from resources or perception.

Changes in key environmental factors as described in chapter III pose major challenges to the individual multinational enterprise, and it has to adopt strategies for adjustment. One implication of these strategies is that production units are becoming more specialised in order to gain economies of scale in global markets. In this context there is a greater need for controlling and monitoring enterprise-wide activities, and further economies may be achieved by centralisation of certain non-production functions such as marketing, purchasing, finance or R & D. Such strategic responses will result in modifications of organisation structure and decision-making. According to the empirical evidence from the large-scale studies conducted by Davidson and Neghandhi and Welge, many multinationals seem to prefer to react with global structures and rather centralised decision-making systems.

As seen in Agthe's study[94], however, reveals that other multinational enterprises are reacting in the opposite way and have adopted what has been called multi-local strategies allowing for rather decentralised systems which have the following principle characteristics: partnership with a local partner in a national firm where the partner should be a business partner rather than a political partner and, according to the national character of the firm, the foreign partner usually takes miniority ownership; the firm is managed like a local firm and, therefore, locals play an important role in the management; by holding minority ownership, the foreign partner gains in flexibility, because its engagement is not subject to consolidation and auditing requirements of the home country, financing is subject to the rules of the respective host country and the financial resources of the foreign partner are not affected; dispersion of foreign investments in various countries in terms of minority ownerships in local enterprises reduces risk; and the interests of foreign minority partners are secured through particular contractual agreements and a corresponding organisation of the management structure. In other words, the concept of a multi-local structure suggests that the enterprise concerned may adopt different approaches to international involvement depending on the circumstances of each situation. Thus, while it may still set up fully or majority owned subsidiaries in some cases, it may also adopt, in others, different forms of involvement, often described in the literature as "new forms" of international investment such as joint ventures, licensing agreements or technology arrangements.

Obviously, the aspects of the international economic situation referred to above have put pressures on a number of multinationals towards adopting global structures and decision-making systems, but these pressures are not always or necessarily ones compelling the adoption of global strategies or, even when they act in that direction, impediments may hinder the realisation of global structures. This also reveals that, in many cases, different options exist for reacting to environmental threats. Management philosophy in the enterprise is likely to be an important factor in determing which option is actually taken in each case.

4. Implications for decision making authority in subsidiaries

This section examines what has been happening to the level of decision making authority in subsidiaries over time and the possible effects on this resulting from changing organisational structures along the two broad stylised tracks referred to above as global and multi-local structures. A first point to note is that the development of an industry through its life cycle may affect relations between a parent company and its subsidiaries engaged in that industry, though whether there is any effect, and if so its extent, will be heavily conditioned by other factors including principally the objectives set for the enterprise as a whole, and the attitude which it takes towards the balance of interests in industries at different stages of maturity. Similar remarks also apply, in many cases, to individual subsidiaries, as was noted above: a parent may watch relatively closely decisions in respect of the development of subsidiaries engaged in newly-developing industries, potentially fast-growing but with as yet no settled competitive environment; be prepared to adopt a more "hands-off" approach in the growth phase; but then again become involved when an industry and the markets which it serves exhibit slower growth or decline. At this latter stage a parent may face very difficult decisions to balance the proposals of subsidiary management for further investment to reinforce its existing position, and its own desire to redeploy resources towards industries and markets offering a prospect of more growth in the medium or longer term.

To the extent that empirical evidence in the literature suggests that some multinational enterprises are moving towards global, integrated structures, it is important to consider the possible impacts on subsidiary autonomy. In general, it is felt that the more integrated the structure the lower will be the local autonomy of the subsidiary. Taking the integrated product structure as an example in order to validate this hypothesis, it is evident that the profit-centre manager who has world-wide responsibility for his product group will have great influence on product-orientated decisions such as pricing, design, advertising, production, R & D, etc. The more influence he has on the decision-making process, the less is the autonomy of local management.

In order to make global strategies and structures effective, a planning and control system has to be implemented that fits the needs of global management. Consequently, the structural and strategic changes demonstrated above should be reflected in the multinational planning and control system. According to studies by Lorange[95], Hawkins and Walter[96] and in Business International[97] a major characteristic of integrated structures is the integration of national and international planning into a global plan. In an integrated product structure, co-ordination of planning is achieved in such a way that the divisions or strategic business units (SBUs) develop world-wide plans using the support of their divisional planning staffs. In matrix structures a balance between product and regional aspects is secured in a way that SBUs develop their product plans, and regional units develop their regional plans. In an interactive procedure, product/region plans are developed, which are aggregated into a corporate plan by corporate headquarters.

The international planning and control system is also affected by various strategic variables. With an increasing degree of internationalisation, the number of regional SBUs which have to be planned in addition to the product-orientated SBUs increases. There is also a positive correlation between internationalisation and the planning horizon. As shown by Arbeitskreis[98], the greater the degree of internationalisation, the longer the planning horizon. In the same study, it was also evident that increasing internationalisation is associated with increasing management time devoted to planning activities. In corporations having a low degree of internationalisation, Schwendiman[99] found that the planning process was rather decentralised, organised according to the bottom-up principle and the responsibility of central planning staffs was rather limited, whereas, as shown by Welge[100], the opposite pattern emerged in highly internationalised companies.

According to a study by Channon and Jalland[101], local responsibility for operative planning increases with increasing product differentiation. Responsibility for strategic planning, however, is centralised at headquarters and control of product-orientated and regional SBUs is achieved by the central allocation of resources. Subsidiaries can be allowed high operative planning autonomy without the parent taking great risk because of the low capital intensity of subsidiaries, non-significant economies of scale of central production as well as necessary responsiveness to local markets, a finding which is also supported by Leksell[102], who found high product differentiation correlated with low process standardisation, because no system would fit the differing requirements of the various product lines.

The extent of internal transfer of goods and services was found to have a very important impact on planning in the studies by Channon and Jalland and Negandhi and Welge referred to above. The more goods and services are transferred between headquarters and subsidiaries, the more centralised is operative and long-range as well as strategic planning. As can be seen from Figures 2, 3 and 4, both the planning and environmental scanning functions are headquarters-orientated. The centralisation of these two functions is more clearly seen with respect to the communication patterns concerning the planning and environmental scanning processes between subsidiaries and their respective headquarters. Among United States multinational enterprises, the nature of communication concerning these two aspects is highly formalised, while German and Japanese companies seem to be moving rapidly to follow the United States example (see Figure 4). In Neghandi and Welge's study, formal communications were transacted as instructions and imperatives rather than constructive exchanges of ideas and information and only one-third of the subsidiaries surveyed felt that their viewpoints were utilised by headquarters.

Figure 2

ENVIRONMENTAL SCANNING AND LONG-RANGE PLANNING AT THE HEADQUARTERS AND SUBSIDIARY LEVELS AMONG THREE TYPES OF MULTINATIONAL CORPORATIONS

1. Environmental Scanning

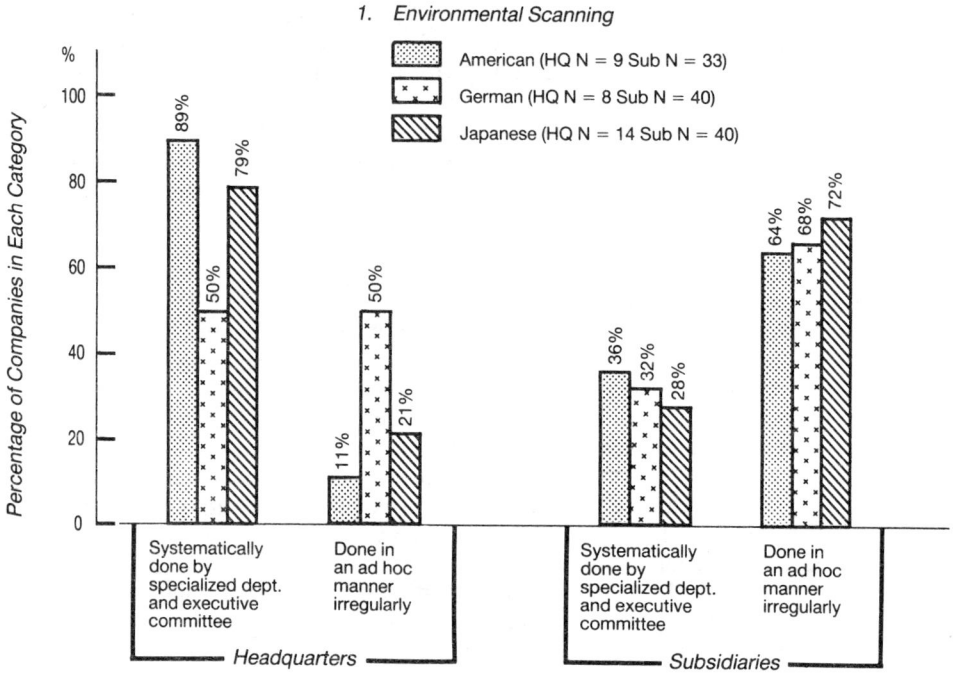

American (HQ N = 9 Sub N = 33)
German (HQ N = 8 Sub N = 40)
Japanese (HQ N = 14 Sub N = 40)

Source: Negandhi and Welge 1984, p. 48.

Note: The figure compares the environmental scanning approach for three groups of multinational enterprises (United States, German and Japanese). In general, it can be seen that scanning at the headquarters level is more often conducted in a systematic manner, whereas scanning at the subsidiary level is more often done in an ad hoc manner. The figure also reveals some differences in these respects between the three groups of enterprises.

Pulling the above indications together, there appears to be a strong tendency for systematic, formalised long-range and strategic integrated planning in multinational enterprises, which, following Dymsza[103], can basically be explained by strategic and structural imperatives. As a consequence of this, Davidson[104] indicates that three characteristics emerge as opposed to firms not adopting such a decision environment; first, planners and analysts play a major role in strategic decisions; secondly, the decision process emphasises systematic analysis of competing strategic options; and thirdly, the context in which decisions are made emphasises the integration of strategic decisions.

Figure 3

LONG-RANGE PLANNING

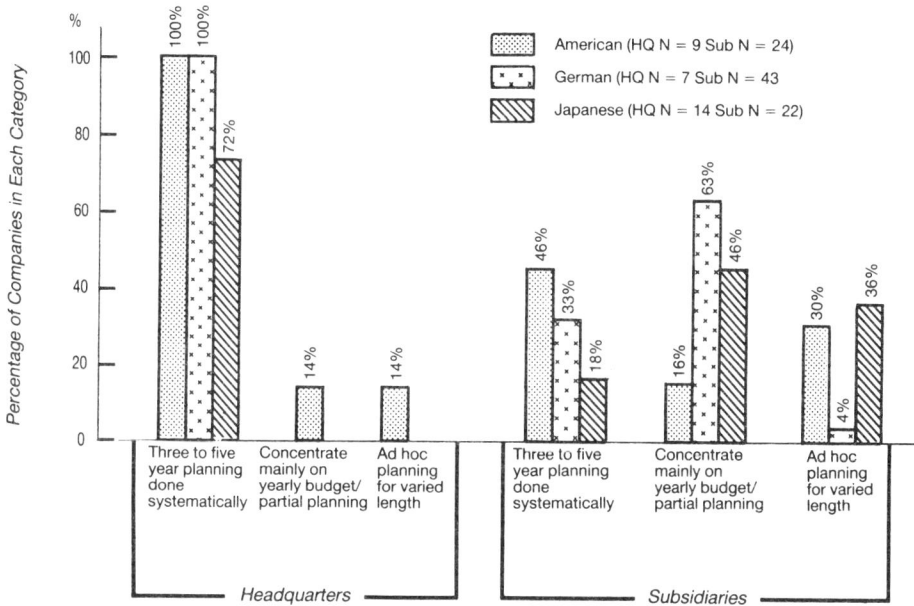

Source: Negandhi and Welge 1984, p. 49.

Note: The figure compares the types of planning conducted by headquarters and subsidiaries for three groups of multinational enterprises (United States, German and Japanese). It can be seen that systematic, 3 to 5 year planning is largely conducted at headquarters level, where there is also little involvement in yearly, ad hoc planning. By comparison, there is much less systematic, 3 to 5 year planning at the subsidiary level, but it is at this level that yearly or ad hoc planning is mostly conducted. The figure also reveals differences in these respects by nationality of the enterprise.

These changes in the decision environment can have significant effects on subsidiary managers. The above-mentioned studies argue that the flexibility, discretion and autonomy of subsidiary managers will be reduced as a result of integrated planning activities. Costs for designing and implementing global information and planning systems may come to exceed those for national organisations. Although it is also true that global firms exist because a network of related subsidiaries is superior to a set of independent entities as a form of economic and strategic organisation, arguments for subsidiary autonomy in some sectors or countries may carry greater weight in the future.

51

Figure 4

INVOLVEMENT OF SUBSIDIARIES IN ENVIRONMENTAL SCANNING AND LONG-RANGE PLANNING PROCESSES

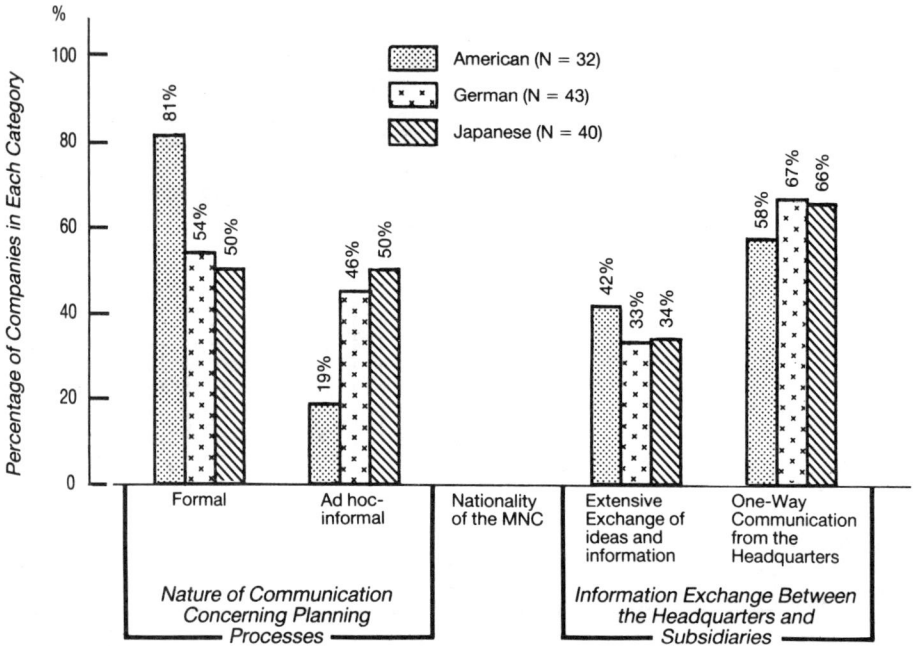

Source: Negandhi and Welge 1984, p. 50.

Note: The figure compares the nature of the communication process between headquarters and subsidiaries and information exchange in the planning and scanning processes between headquarters and subsidiaries in three groups of multinational enterprises (United States, German and Japanese). In general, formal communication processes dominate informal, ad hoc ones, although there are important differences between United States firms on the one hand and German and Japanese firms on the other. Despite this difference, the figure shows, however, little differences by nationality as to the nature of information exchange where, for the majority of the firms in each group, this takes the form of a one-way exchange, from the headquarters to the subsidiary so that, on average, about two-thirds of the subsidiaries have relatively little input into these processes in the companies investigated.

On the face of it, moves in organisational structure towards the multi-local approach might suggest a generally higher level of decision making autonomy at the level of the foreign operation, either by design or necessity. This hypothesis stems from the fact that the forms of international involvement which go hand in hand with a multi-local structure may often be associated with minority or even non-equity positions and it has been argued in chapter III that, other things being equal, the lower is the parent company's stake in the foreign operation the more it may be willing to or have to accept reduced control. It is equally clear, however, and as recalled in the discussion in chapter III of the possible impacts on structure resulting from local pressures and demands, that, in moving away from wholly owned subsidiaries to other forms of involvement, companies can organise this involvement in a number of ways to maintain the desired level of control or at least to minimise its dilution.

From the above, it does seem clear that a tendency for one group of multinational enterprises is that they are moving towards or strengthening integrated structures in the context of global strategies. As indicated earlier in this report, such moves are likely to be accompanied by the greater concentration of decision making power in a number of strategic areas at the parent level, but equally with greater autonomy at the subsidiary level for others. It may be that, as suggested by the Conference Board study[105], for firms moving in this direction, decision areas already relatively centralised may be becoming more so and vice versa. As the subsidiary becomes more integrated into the overall network of activities of the enterprise as a whole it not only becomes of greater importance to the parent but it may equally increase its voice in decision areas which are of direct concern to ensure the maintenance of local flexibility despite the greater need for oversight.

Moves towards global integration are of course not the only manner in which organisational structures have been changing. Already in a 1981 OECD study of foreign direct investment trends[106] it was noted that many of the forms of international involvement which appear to be associated with the development of multi-local structures had assumed importance, a trend which has been confirmed in the recently updated version of that study[107]. As in the case for firms adopting global strategies, the implications for real subsidiary autonomy, in enterprises moving towards multi-local strategies are, as noted above, not all that straightforward either. Furthermore, it may not be entirely appropriate to regard these two broad types of organisational responses as polar opposites. Indeed, some authors have suggested that global structures may in fact end up representing in many cases, in a period of relatively slow growth and intense restructuring, a transitional phase in the direction of multi-local structures rather than a definitive form of response.

Chapter V

SUMMARY AND CONCLUSIONS

The topic of the present study – features and trends in the organisational structures of multinational enterprises – has been chosen in relation to the OECD Guidelines for Multinational Enterprises which, as noted in Chapter I, address a number of recommendations to enterprises which are pertinant to their organisational structure. Also, the way in which multinational enterprises are structured is to some extent relevant to the manner in which enterprises can follow these recommendations.

It is evident from this study that organisational structures and parent-subsidiary relationships in multinational enterprises, influenced as they are by a large variety of forces, are often complex and fluid. The position of subsidiaries, especially foreign located subsidiaries in the enterprise as whole, particularly with respect to the level of decision making authority, is often discussed in the context of the need for supervision and flexibility. Supervision, associated with more centralised control, in most of the studies examined is required in large and complex enterprises to ensure coordination of activities and the compatibility of subsidiaries' activities with overall company strategy. Flexibility, generally associated with decentralised decision making, concerns the need for appropriate and often rapid actions to meet changing circumstances, where knowledge and experience of the local situation are normally key requirements. The organisational structures of multinational enterprises can be seen as the means by which such enterprises manage these often competing forces.

In examining actual patterns of behaviour, and the factors determining these patterns, it is important to bear in mind a number of general points. For example, there are many different types of multinational enterprises (e.g., with respect to size, complexity, degree of internationality), establishment or expansion of foreign operations can take various forms (e.g., greenfield investment, acquisition), and the nature of involvement can range from full or majority ownership to minority or even zero equity participation.

The exercise of parent authority over a subsidiary's activities may range from direct instruction to passive ratification, while the desired level of oversight can be achieved in various ways such as the use of financial thresholds, production specificaitons and standardised methods. More indirect means may include the positioning of key personnel and the use of intra-company visits. In the end, however, the question of how management at different levels of the organisational structure interact, particularly with respect to strategic decisions, may be more important than that of whether the parent or the subsidiary takes a particular decision.

In studies examining decision making patterns in multinational enterprises, one aspect that stands out is the distinction between strategic decisions, with a generally high level of parent involvement, and operational decisions, usually associated with high levels of subsidiary decision making authority. Within this broad pattern, there are, of course, important differences between multinational enterprises with respect to the degree of centralisation of a particular decision area and how this is achieved. In addition, strategic and operational decisions are generally linked in that, for example, major capital expenditure decisions such as opening a new plant or undertaking a large expansion affect operational decisions such as employment levels. Thus, while central control in one decision area does not imply similar control in a different area, this must be seen in the perspective of the links that exist between different decision areas.

A large variety of factors affect the organisational structures chosen by multinational enterprises and the position of the subsidiary in the enterprise as a whole. One set of factors concerns characteristics of the corporation, such as those related to the parent or group as a whole (e.g., sector, nationality, size, degree of internationalisation, corporate strategy), to specific features of the subsidiary (e.g., country of location, size, age, performance), or to the nature of links (ownership, interdependence) between parent and subsidiary. The other main set of factors concerns the environment in which the enterprise operates, including the economic situation (e.g., market situation, uncertainty and instability), competition, technology (e.g., the role of advanced information technology in facilitating the adoption of a given organisational structure) and the role of host government policies (particularly as they address the position of local subsidiaries via preconditions and/or performance requirements). Outside these two broad sets of forces, the role played by more intangible aspects such as tradition, business philosophy and personalities should not be underemphasized.

As the above forces change over time, and many of them have changed quite dramatically over the last decade or so, it can be expected that these will be associated with changes in what is felt to be the most suitable organisational structure. Clearly, and given the diversity in multinational enterprises with respect to their internal features and the nature of their market situations, changes in organisational structure in any one single direction cannot be expected. There has, however, been considerable focus on two broad approaches – integrated global structures and multi-local structures. The former approach is associated with the enterprise operating in global markets and taking a world wide view of its activities because of the growing need for integration and coordination as well as to realise important economies from this type of structure. By comparison, multi-local structures are associated with differing approaches to international involvement including those often described as "new forms" of international investment, depending on the circumstances of each case. These two broad approaches should not be seen as separate or polar opposites, and it has been suggested that in an environment characterised by low growth, high uncertainty and intense structural change, global structures may end up representing, in many cases, a transitional form of organisational structure rather than a definitive response.

NOTES AND REFERENCES

1. See, International Investment and Multinational Enterprises: The OECD Guidelines for Multinational Enterprises, OECD, 1986, paragraph 8.

2. International Investment and Multinational Enterprises: Review of the 1976 Declaration and Decisions. OECD, 1979.

3. International Investment and Multinational Enterprises: The 1984 Review of the 1976 Declaration and Decisions. OECD, 1984.

4. OECD (1986) *op. cit.* paragraphs 65 and 66.

5. OECD (1986) *op. cit.*, paragraphs 80 and 81.

6. See, in particular, Oman, C., New Forms of International Investment in Developing Countries. OECD, 1984.

7. Brooke, M.Z. and Black, M.: The Autonomy of the Foreign Subsidiary: A Progress Report on Research. In: International STudies in Management and Organisations, Vol. 6, 1976, pp. 11-26.

8. The Conference Board Operating Foreign Subsidiaries: How Independent Can They be? Report No. 836, 1983.

9. Ghertman, M.: Decision making in Multinational Enterprises: Concepts and Research Approaches. Working Paper No. 31. ILO, Geneva, 1984.

10. Negandhi, A.R. and Welge, M.K.: Beyond Theory Z: Global Rationalisation Strategies of American, German and Japanese Multinational Companies. Greenwich: JAI Press 1984.

11. Welge, M.K.: Decision Making in German Multinationals and its Impact on External Relationships. In: Governments and Multinationals. The Policy of Control Versus Autonomy, Ed. by W.H. Goldberg. Cambridge: Oelgeschlager, Gunn & Hain 1983, pp. 57-77.

12. Alsegg, R.J.: Control Relationships Between American Corporations and Their European Subsidiaries. AMA Research Study 107. American Management Association Inc. 1971.

13. Abell, P.: Parent Companies Control of Subsidiaries. In: Multinational Business, Heft 1, 1974, pp. 11-22.

14. Hedlund, G.: Autonomy of Subsidiaries and Formalisation of Headquarter-Subsidiary Relationships in Swedish Multinational Enterprises. In: The Management of Headquarters-Subsidiary Relationships in Multinational Corporations ed. by L. Otterbeck, Stockholm: Gover 1981, pp. 25-78.

15. Yunker, P.J.: A Survey Study of Subsidiary Autonomy Performance Evaluation and Transfer Pricing in Multinational Corporations. In: Columbia Journal of World Business, Vol. 17, 1983, No. 3, pp. 51-64.

16. Brandt, W. and Hulbert, J.M.: Headquarter Guidance in Marketing Strategy in the Multinational Subsidiary. In: Columbia Journal of World Business, Vol. 12, 1977, pp. 7-14.

17. Alpander, G.G.: Multinational Corporations. Homebase-Affiliate Relations. In: California Management Review, Vol. 20, 1978, pp. 47-56.

18. The Conference Board (1983) *op. cit.*

19. Young, S., Hood, N. and Hamill, J.: Decision Making in Foreign Owned Multinational Subsidiaries in the United Kingdom. Working Paper No. 35, ILO 1985.

20. Steuer, M.D. *et al.:* The Impact of Foreign Direct Investment on the United Kingdom. HMSO, 1973.

21. Hood, N. and Young, S.: Multinational Investment Strategies in the British Isles: A Study of Multinational Enterprises in the Assisted Areas and the Republic of Ireland. HMSO, 1983.

22. Hamill, J.: The Labour Relations Practices of Foreign Owned and Indigenous Firms. Employee Relations 5(1), 1983.

23. Van Den Bulke, D. and Halsberghe, E.: Employment Decision Making in Multinational Enterprises: Survey Results for Belgium, Working Paper No. 32, ILO, 1984.

24. Ghertman, M. (1984) *op. cit.*

25. Garnier, G.A.: Context and Decision-Making Autonomy in the Foreign Affiliates of United States Multinational Corporations. In: Academy of Management Journal, Vol. 25, 1982, pp. 893-908.

26. Egelhoff, W.G.: Patterns of Control in United States, United Kingdom and European Multinational Corporations. In: Journal of International Business Studies, Vol. 15, 1984, pp. 73-84.

27. Alsegg, R.J., (1971) *op. cit.*

28. Garnier, G.A., (1982) *op. cit.*

29. Brooke, M.Z. and Remmers, H.L.: International Management and Business Policy. Boston: Houghton Mifflin Company 1978.

30. Brandt, W. and Hulbert, J.M. (1977) *op. cit.*

31. Kenter, M.E.: Die Steuerung ausländischer Tochtergesellschaften. Instrumente und Effizienz. Frankfurt/Main-Bern-New York: P. Lang 1985.

32. Kenter, M.E. and Welge, M.K.: Die Reintegration von Stammhausdelegierten – Ergebnisse einer explorativen empirischen Untersuchung. In: Personelle Aspekte im internationalen Management, ed. by E. Dülfer, Berlin: E. Schmidt 1983, pp. 173-200.

33. Kenter, M.E., (1985) *op. cit.*

34. Gaydoul, P.: Controlling in der deutschen Unternehmenspraxis. Darmstadt 1980.

35. Garnier, G.A., (1982) *op. cit.*

36. The Conference Board (1983) *op. cit.*

37. Hedlund, G. (1981) *op. cit.*

38. Negandhi, A.R. and Welge, M.K. (1984) *op. cit.*

39. Brandt, W. and Holbert, J.M. (1977) *op. cit.*

40. Ergas, H. and Reid, A. Transborder Data Flows in Multinational Enterprises: The Results of a joint BIAC/OECD Survey and Interview with Firms, in Transborder Data Flows: Proceedings of an OECD Conference, Chapter III, North Holland, 1985.

41. Young, S., Hood, N. and Hamill, J. (1985) *op. cit.*

42. Van Den Bulke, D. and Halsberghe, E. (1984) *op. cit.*

43. Dunning, J. H. Decision Making Structures in U.S., and Japanese Manufacturing Affiliates in the United Kingdom: Some similarities and Contrasts, Working Paper No. 41, ILO, 1986.

44. Egelhoff, W.G. (1984) *op. cit.*

45. Brandt, W. and Hulbert, J.M. (1977) *op. cit.*

46. Ouchi, W.G.: Theory Z. How American Business Can Meet the Japanese Challenge, Reading, Mass.: Addisen-Wesley 1981.

47. Cray, D.: Control and Co-ordination in Multinational Corporations. In: Journal of International Business Studies, Vol. 15, 1984, pp. 85-98.

48. Picard, J.: Factors of Variance in Multinational Marketing Control. In: Recent Research on the Internationalisation of Business – Proceedings from the Annual Meeting of the European Business Association in Uppsala 1977, ed. by L.G. Mattson, A.F. Wiedersheim-Paul, Uppsala 1979, pp. 220-232.

49. Yunker, P.G. (1983) op. cit.

50. Abell, P. (1974) op. cit.

51. Brooke, M.Z. and Remmers, H.L. (1978) op. cit.

52. Kenter, M.E. (1985) op. cit.

53. Ghertman, M. (1984) op. cit.

54. Zeira, Y. and Shenkar, O. Personnel Decision Making in Wholly Owned Foreign Subsidiaries and in International Joint Ventures. Working Paper No. 45, ILO, 1986.

55. Young, S., Hood, N. and Hammil, J. (1985) op. cit.

56. Kenter, M.E. (1985) op. cit.

57. Brooke, M.Z. and Remmers, H.L. (1978) op. cit.

58. Garnier, G.A. (1982) op. cit.

59. Welge, M.K.: Entscheidungsprozesse in komplexen, international tätigen Unternehmungen. In: Aeitschrift für Betriebswirtschaft, Vol. 52, 1982, pp. 810-833.

60. Hedlund, G. (1981) op. cit.

61. Picard, J. (1979) op. cit.

62. Cray, D. (1984) op. cit.

63. Garnier, G.A. (1982) op. cit.

64. Welge, M.K. (1983) op. cit.

65. Alsegg, R.J., (1971) op. cit.

66. Cray, D. (1984) op. cit.

67. Egelhoff, W. G. (1984) op. cit.

68. Picard, J. (1979) op. cit.

69. Hedlund, G. (1981) op. cit.

70. Youssef, S.M.: Contextual Factors influencing Control Strategy of Multinational Corporations. In: Academy of Management Journal, Vol. 18, 1975, No. 1, pp. 136-143.

71. Picard, J. (1979) op. cit.

72. Brooke, M.Z. and Black, M. (1976) op. cit.

73. Positive Adjustment Policies: Managing Structural Change, OECD, 1983.

74. Dunning, J.H. (1986) op. cit.

75. Doz, Y.L., Strategic Management in Multinational Companies. Sloan Management Review, Winter 1980.

76. Ergas, H. and Reid, A. (1985) op. cit.

77. See Franko, L.G., The European Multinationals, 1978 and Brooke, M. and Remmers, L. (1978) op. cit.

78. International Investment and Multinational Enterprises: Structural Adjustment and Multinational Enterprises. OECD, 1985.

79. International Investment and Multinational Enterprises: Investment Incentives and Disincentives and the International Investment Process. OECD, 1983.

80. The Conference Board (1983) *op. cit.*

81. Alsegg, R.G. (1971) *op. cit.*

82. Barlow, E.R.: Management of Foreign Manufacturing Subsidiaries, Boston 1953.

83. Welge, M.K. (1982) *op. cit.*

84. Young, S., Hood, N. and Hamill, J. (1985) *op. cit.*

85. The Conference Board (1983) *op. cit.*

86. Chandler, A.D.: Strategy and Structure. Cambridge: The MIT Press 1962.

87. Brooke, M.W. and Remmers, H.L. (1978) *op. cit.*

88. Stopford, J.M. and Wells, L.T.: Managing the Multinational Enterprise. New York: Basic Books 1972.

89. Channon, D.F.: The Strategy and Structure of British Enterprise. London: MacMillan 1973.

90. Franko, L.G. (1978) *op. cit.*

91. Yoshino, M.Y.: Japan's Multinational Enterprises. Cambridge: Harvard University Press 1976.

92. Davidson, W.H.: Global Strategic Management. New York: John Wiley 1982.

93. Porter, M. E., Competitive Strategy, New York, the Free Press, 1980.

94. Aghte, K.E.: "Multi-local" statt "Multi-national" als strategisches Konzept eines internationalen Unternehmens. In: Internationalisierung der Unternehmung als Problem der Betriebswirtschaftslehre, ed. by W. Lück and V. Trommsdorff. Berlin: Schmidt Verlag 1982, pp. 147-170.

95. Lorange, P.: A Framework for Strategic Planning in Multinational Corporations. In: Long-Range Planning, Vol. 9, 1976, pp. 30-37.

96. Hawkins, R.G. and Walter, I.: Planning Multinational Operations. In: Handbook of Organisational Design, Vol. 1, ed. by P.C. Nystroem and W.H. Starbuck. New York: Oxford University Press, 1981, pp. 253-267.

97. Business International Corporation: Strategic Planning for International Corporations. New York, 1979.

98. Arbeitskreis: "Organisation international tätiger Unternehmen" der Schmalenbach-Gesellschaft: Organisation des Planungsprozesses in international tätigen Unternehmen. In: Seitschrift für betriebswirtschaftliche Forschung, Vol. 31, 1979, pp. 25-30.

99. Schwendiman, J.S.: Strategic and Long-Range Planning for the Multinational Corporation. New York: Praeger 1973.

100. Welge, M.K. (1983) *op. cit.*

101. Channon, D.F. and Jalland, M.: Multinational Strategic Planning. London: MacMillan 1979.

102. Leksell, L.: Headquarter-Subsidiary Relationships in Multinational Corporations. PhD Dissertation, University of Stockholm 1981.

103. Dymsza, W.A.: Global Strategic Planning: A model and Recent Developments. In: Journal of International Business Studies, Vol. 15, 1984, pp. 169-183.

104. Davidson, W.H. (1982) *op. cit.*

105. The Conference Board (1983) *op cit.*

106. International Investment and Multinational Enterprises: Recent International Direct Investment Trends. OECD, 1981.

107. International Investment and Multinational Enterprises: Recent Trends in Foreign Direct Investment. OECD, 1987.

WHERE TO OBTAIN OECD PUBLICATIONS
OÙ OBTENIR LES PUBLICATIONS DE L'OCDE

ARGENTINA - ARGENTINE
Carlos Hirsch S.R.L.,
Florida 165, 4º Piso,
(Galeria Guemes) 1333 Buenos Aires
Tel. 33.1787.2391 y 30.7122

AUSTRALIA - AUSTRALIE
D.A. Book (Aust.) Pty. Ltd.
11-13 Station Street (P.O. Box 163)
Mitcham, Vic. 3132   Tel. (03) 873 4411

AUSTRIA - AUTRICHE
OECD Publications and Information Centre,
4 Simrockstrasse,
5300 Bonn (Germany)   Tel. (0228) 21.60.45
Gerold & Co., Graben 31, Wien 1 Tel. 52.22.35

BELGIUM - BELGIQUE
Jean de Lannoy,
avenue du Roi 202
B-1060 Bruxelles   Tel. (02) 538.51.69

CANADA
Renouf Publishing Company Ltd/
Éditions Renouf Ltée,
1294 Algoma Road, Ottawa, Ont. K1B 3W8
Tel: (613) 741-4333
Toll Free/Sans Frais:
Ontario, Quebec, Maritimes:
1-800-267-1805
Western Canada, Newfoundland:
1-800-267-1826
Stores/Magasins:
61 rue Sparks St., Ottawa, Ont. K1P 5A6
Tel: (613) 238-8985
211 rue Yonge St., Toronto, Ont. M5B 1M4
Tel: (416) 363-3171

DENMARK - DANEMARK
Munksgaard Export and Subscription Service
35, Nørre Søgade, DK-1370 København K
Tel. +45.1.12.85.70

FINLAND - FINLANDE
Akateeminen Kirjakauppa,
Keskuskatu 1, 00100 Helsinki 10 Tel. 0.12141

FRANCE
OCDE/OECD
Mail Orders/Commandes par correspondance :
2, rue André-Pascal,
75775 Paris Cedex 16
Tel. (1) 45.24.82.00
Bookshop/Librairie : 33, rue Octave-Feuillet
75016 Paris
Tel. (1) 45.24.81.67 or/ou (1) 45.24.81.81
Librairie de l'Université,
12a, rue Nazareth,
13602 Aix-en-Provence   Tel. 42.26.18.08

GERMANY - ALLEMAGNE
OECD Publications and Information Centre,
4 Simrockstrasse,
5300 Bonn   Tel. (0228) 21.60.45

GREECE - GRÈCE
Librairie Kauffmann,
28, rue du Stade, 105 64 Athens Tel. 322.21.60

HONG KONG
Government Information Services,
Publications (Sales) Office,
Information Services Department
No. 1, Battery Path, Central

ICELAND - ISLANDE
Snæbjörn Jónsson & Co., h.f.,
Hafnarstræti 4 & 9,
P.O.B. 1131 – Reykjavik
Tel. 13133/14281/11936

INDIA - INDE
Oxford Book and Stationery Co.,
Scindia House, New Delhi 1 Tel. 331.5896/5308
17 Park St., Calcutta 700016   Tel. 240832

INDONESIA - INDONÉSIE
Pdii-Lipi, P.O. Box 3065/JKT.Jakarta
Tel. 583467

IRELAND - IRLANDE
TDC Publishers - Library Suppliers,
12 North Frederick Street, Dublin 1
Tel. 744835-749677

ITALY - ITALIE
Libreria Commissionaria Sansoni,
Via Lamarmora 45, 50121 Firenze
Tel. 579751/584468
Via Bartolini 29, 20155 Milano   Tel. 365083
Editrice e Libreria Herder,
Piazza Montecitorio 120, 00186 Roma
Tel. 6794628
Libreria Hœpli,
Via Hœpli 5, 20121 Milano   Tel. 865446
Libreria Scientifica
Dott. Lucio de Biasio "Aeiou"
Via Meravigli 16, 20123 Milano   Tel. 807679
Libreria Lattes,
Via Garibaldi 3, 10122 Torino   Tel. 519274
La diffusione delle edizioni OCSE è inoltre
assicurata dalle migliori librerie nelle città più
importanti.

JAPAN - JAPON
OECD Publications and Information Centre,
Landic Akasaka Bldg., 2-3-4 Akasaka,
Minato-ku, Tokyo 107   Tel. 586.2016

KOREA - CORÉE
Kyobo Book Centre Co. Ltd.
P.O.Box: Kwang Hwa Moon 1658,
Seoul   Tel. (REP) 730.78.91

LEBANON - LIBAN
Documenta Scientifica/Redico,
Edison Building, Bliss St.,
P.O.B. 5641, Beirut   Tel. 354429-344425

MALAYSIA - MALAISIE
University of Malaya Co-operative Bookshop
Ltd.,
P.O.Box 1127, Jalan Pantai Baru,
Kuala Lumpur   Tel. 577701/577072

NETHERLANDS - PAYS-BAS
Staatsuitgeverij
Chr. Plantijnstraat, 2 Postbus 20014
2500 EA S-Gravenhage   Tel. 070-789911
Voor bestellingen: Tel. 070-789880

NEW ZEALAND - NOUVELLE-ZÉLANDE
Government Printing Office Bookshops:
Auckland: Retail Bookshop, 25 Rutland Stseet,
Mail Orders, 85 Beach Road
Private Bag C.P.O.
Hamilton: Retail: Ward Street,
Mail Orders, P.O. Box 857
Wellington: Retail, Mulgrave Street, (Head
Office)
Cubacade World Trade Centre,
Mail Orders, Private Bag
Christchurch: Retail, 159 Hereford Street,
Mail Orders, Private Bag
Dunedin: Retail, Princes Street,
Mail Orders, P.O. Box 1104

NORWAY - NORVÈGE
Tanum-Karl Johan
Karl Johans gate 43, Oslo 1
PB 1177 Sentrum, 0107 Oslo 1 Tel. (02) 42.93.10

PAKISTAN
Mirza Book Agency
65 Shahrah Quaid-E-Azam, Lahore 3 Tel. 66839

PORTUGAL
Livraria Portugal,
Rua do Carmo 70-74, 1117 Lisboa Codex
Tel. 360582/3

SINGAPORE - SINGAPOUR
Information Publications Pte Ltd
Pei-Fu Industrial Building,
24 New Industrial Road No. 02-06
Singapore 1953   Tel. 2831786, 2831798

SPAIN - ESPAGNE
Mundi-Prensa Libros, S.A.,
Castelló 37, Apartado 1223, Madrid-28001
Tel. 431.33.99
Libreria Bosch, Ronda Universidad 11,
Barcelona 7   Tel. 317.53.08/317.53.58

SWEDEN - SUÈDE
AB CE Fritzes Kungl. Hovbokhandel,
Box 16356, S 103 27 STH,
Regeringsgatan 12,
DS Stockholm   Tel. (08) 23.89.00
Subscription Agency/Abonnements:
Wennergren-Williams AB,
Box 30004, S104 25 Stockholm Tel. (08)54.12.00

SWITZERLAND - SUISSE
OECD Publications and Information Centre,
4 Simrockstrasse,
5300 Bonn (Germany)   Tel. (0228) 21.60.45
Librairie Payot,
6 rue Grenus, 1211 Genève 11
Tel. (022) 31.89.50

United Nations Bookshop/
Librairie des Nations-Unies
Palais des Nations,
1211 – Geneva 10
Tel. 022-34-60-11 (ext. 48 72)

TAIWAN - FORMOSE
Good Faith Worldwide Int'l Co., Ltd.
9th floor, No. 118, Sec.2
Chung Hsiao E. Road
Taipei   Tel. 391.7396/391.7397

THAILAND - THAILANDE
Suksit Siam Co., Ltd.,
1715 Rama IV Rd.,
Samyam Bangkok 5   Tel. 2511630

TURKEY - TURQUIE
Kültur Yayinlari Is-Türk Ltd. Sti.
Atatürk Bulvari No: 191/Kat. 21
Kavaklidere/Ankara   Tel. 25.07.60
Dolmabahce Cad. No: 29
Besiktas/Istanbul   Tel. 160.71.88

UNITED KINGDOM - ROYAUME-UNI
H.M. Stationery Office,
Postal orders only: (01)211-5656
P.O.B. 276, London SW8 5DT
Telephone orders: (01) 622.3316, or
Personal callers:
49 High Holborn, London WC1V 6HB
Branches at: Belfast, Birmingham,
Bristol, Edinburgh, Manchester

UNITED STATES - ÉTATS-UNIS
OECD Publications and Information Centre,
2001 L Street, N.W., Suite 700,
Washington, D.C. 20036 - 4095
Tel. (202) 785.6323

VENEZUELA
Libreria del Este,
Avda F. Miranda 52, Aptdo. 60337,
Edificio Galipan, Caracas 106
Tel. 32.23.01/33.26.04/31.58.38

YUGOSLAVIA - YOUGOSLAVIE
Jugoslovenska Knjiga, Knez Mihajlova 2,
P.O.B. 36, Beograd   Tel. 621.992

Orders and inquiries from countries where
Distributors have not yet been appointed should be
sent to:
OECD, Publications Service, Sales and
Distribution Division, 2, rue André-Pascal, 75775
PARIS CEDEX 16.

Les commandes provenant de pays où l'OCDE n'a
pas encore désigné de distributeur peuvent être
adressées à :
OCDE, Service des Publications. Division des
Ventes et Distribution. 2. rue André-Pascal. 75775
PARIS CEDEX 16.

71055-09-1987

OECD PUBLICATIONS, 2, rue André-Pascal, 75775 PARIS CEDEX 16 - No. 42225 1987
PRINTED IN FRANCE
(21 87 12 1) ISBN 92-64-13030-6